Switching in IP Networks:

IP Switching, Tag Switching, and Related Technologies

The Morgan Kaufmann Series in Networking
Series Editor, David Clark

Switching in IP Networks:

IP Switching, Tag Switching, and Related Technologies

Bruce Davie

Paul Doolan

Yakov Rekhter

Morgan Kaufmann Publishers, Inc.
San Francisco, California

Sponsoring Editor	Jennifer Mann
Director of Production and Manufacturing	Yonie Overton
Production Editor	Edward Wade
Production Assistant	Pamela Sullivan
Editorial Assistant	Karyn Johnson
Cover Design	Ross Carron Design
Text Design and Composition	Sybil Ihrig, Helios Productions
Illustration	John Wincek
Copyeditor	Erin Milnes
Proofreader	Ken DellaPenta
Indexer	Steve Rath
Cover Photograph	Chris Cheadle, Tony Stone Images
Printer	Courier Corporation

Morgan Kaufmann Publishers, Inc.
Editorial and Sales Office
340 Pine Street, Sixth Floor
San Francisco, CA 94104-3205
USA
Telephone   415-392-2665
Facsimile   415-982-2665
Email   mkp@mkp.com
Web site   *www.mkp.com*
Order toll free 800-745-7323

Library of Congress Cataloging-in-Publication Data

Davie, Bruce S.
     Switching in IP networks : IP switching, tag switching, and
related technologies / Bruce Davie, Paul Doolan, Yakov Rekhter.
          p.   cm.
     Includes bibliographical references and index.
     ISBN 1-55860-505-3
     1. Internet (Computer network) 2. Telecommunication—Switching
systems. 3. Internetworking (Telecommunication) I. Doolan, Paul,
1956– . II. Rekhter, Yakov. III. Title.
TK5105.875.I57.D38   1998   98-4558
004.6'6--dc21   CP

Contents

Preface

IP Switching, Tag Switching, Multiprotocol Label Switching, and various similar technologies have been among the hottest topics in networking in recent years. The interest in such technologies can be traced in part to the huge success of the Internet and its core protocol, IP, and the desire to build larger, faster IP networks. However, the volume of words penned on these topics in the trade press has done little to dispel the confusion that surrounds them. There is confusion in many areas. How do these technologies work? What are the differences between them? How do they perform in a real network? Will any of them have an impact on the marketplace, or will existing technologies such as IP routing and ATM switching meet our networking needs for the foreseeable future? It is the goal of this book to provide answers to these questions.

Much of the book is devoted to an explanation of how the various new technologies work. We chose four related approaches for detailed examination: IP Switching from Ipsilon, Tag Switching from Cisco Systems, Toshiba's Cell Switching Router (CSR), and IBM's Aggregate Route-based IP Switching (ARIS). These are all examples of the general technique called *label switching*. All of them enable the forwarding of IP packets under the control of standard IP routing algorithms. What distinguishes them from conventional routing is the fact that the forwarding (or switching) process does not use the IP packet header directly; instead, a short, fixed-length label is used to enable packet forwarding.

The reason for choosing to explore and compare these four approaches in particular is that they are the most well known, with the most potential to affect the standards and the market-place. They also represent a good cross section of the field.

In addition to explaining the technical details of how the various schemes work, we have examined the problems that each of them attempts to solve. While it might at first appear that they are all trying to solve one problem—performance—this in fact is just a small piece of the puzzle. Label switching promises to address a much wider range of issues, including the scalability and evolution of IP networks.

Because the approaches to label switching represent different points in a design space, an important goal of this book is to examine the merits of the different design decisions that each team has made. Thus, throughout the book we try to answer the question of why a particular approach works the way it does and to describe the consequences of each major design decision. We have endeavored to show the strengths and weaknesses of each approach. Each chapter that describes a particular approach was reviewed by one or more members of the team that invented it; thus, we believe that the analysis is as technically accurate and fair as possible.

We have tried to make this book accessible to a wide audience. It has been necessary to assume a certain amount of knowledge of IP routing on the part of the reader, but we have provided some background in this area where appropriate. More advanced readers should not hesitate to skim sections that look like standard discussions of routing. Similarly, some fairly advanced capabilities are described in some sections, and readers with a less strong background in routing should not feel ashamed to skip through those sections.

We hope the book will be of value to network designers and engineers who need to understand enough about label switching technology to determine whether it is a possible candidate for deployment in their networks. You should find enough here to gain an understanding of the strengths and weaknesses of label switching compared to conventional techniques and to weigh the different products against each other. The information here will make it easier to understand the detailed technical material that can be found in Internet Drafts, Requests for Comments (RFCs), and in the literature provided by the various companies. You may also gain a sense of whether to go with one vendor's proprietary approach now or to wait for a standard to emerge in the future.

Organization of This Book

The chapters of this book divide into three groups:

- Introduction and Overview: Chapters 1 and 2
- Details of Four Approaches: Chapters 3 through 6
- Comparison and Combination: Chapters 7 and 8

In the first chapter, we examine why it was necessary to invent various flavors of label switching. We discuss the numerous problems that label switching purports to solve. There is also a brief history of the inventions and announcements that made this topic the focus of so much attention. Chapter 2 describes the overall architectural issues that pertain to the whole area of label switching. There are certain fundamental similarities between all the approaches, such as the forwarding algorithm and use of IP control protocols. Also, the designers of any approach must make some of the same key architectural choices, for example, between control-driven and data-driven label assignment.

Chapters 3 through 6 provide detailed descriptions of each of the four approaches mentioned above: CSR, IP Switching, Tag Switching, and ARIS. The chapters are arranged in chronological order of publication of the four schemes. Each chapter begins with an overview of the approach and the architectural choices that its designers have made, before describing the detailed mechanisms and protocols that are used. There is a concluding discussion of the most notable characteristics of the approach in question. Each of these chapters has been reviewed for technical accuracy and objectivity by one of the members of the team that designed the approach in question.

In Chapter 7 we compare all the different approaches. We examine the strengths and weaknesses of each and consider the environments in which one approach or the other might be most suitable. Of course, there are some environments in which none of these approaches may be suitable, but where a more conventional technique may be appropriate.

Finally, Chapter 8 presents the Multiprotocol Label Switching (MPLS) standard being developed in the major Internet standards body, the Internet Engineering Task Force (IETF). More precisely, we present the latest snapshot of the standard-in-progress that we can provide at the time of writing. MPLS represents a compromise between several of the approaches described in the earlier parts of the book; we will see how the strengths of different techniques have been incorporated into the standard.

Throughout the book, but primarily in Chapters 2 and 7, we have made comments about the strengths and weaknesses of different approaches and the wisdom of the various design decisions that each approach has made. As much as possible, we have tried to be objective and unbiased in our analysis. Because we, the authors, have also been involved as designers of one approach and participants in the standards process, it is inevitable that we favor some design choices over others. Probably no author could be completely neutral when discussing such matters. However, we have endeavored to present the different approaches and comparative arguments in a way such that readers can draw their own conclusions. Our reviewers helped enormously in keeping the discussion as objective as possible.

Acknowledgments

We are greatly indebted to those who reviewed all or part of this book. We especially appreciated the neutral viewpoints provided by many of the reviewers. Robert Beliveau, Maureen Lecuona, and Mike Minnich provided useful feedback on the initial outline. Substantial review of the manuscript was provided by John Brassil, Juha Heinanen, Charles Rogers, Lee Rothstein, and Luis Zapata. Hiroshi Esaki of Toshiba reviewed the chapter on CSR; Peter Newman and Greg Minshall (both, at the time, from Ipsilon) reviewed the IP Switching chapter; and Richard Woundy, of American Internet, reviewed the ARIS chapter. We appreciate all the helpful suggestions and corrections provided by these people; they have greatly enhanced the value of the book.

We also wish to thank everyone at Morgan Kaufmann Publishers who made this book possible. The encouragement of our editor, Jennifer Mann, and the considerable support of her assistant, Karyn Johnson, made the whole process almost enjoyable at times. The entertainment budget of MKP, as administered by Jennifer, livened up many an otherwise dull conference.

The fact that we were able to write this book at all is in large part due to the flexibility and generosity of our employers, Cisco Systems (in Paul's case, both Cisco and Ennovate Networks). As well as providing us all with "day jobs" during the writing of the book, they gave us the chance to work together on the development of label switching technology. We thank them for this opportunity.

Finally, none of us could have survived the challenge of writing a book in our spare time without the support and understanding of our families, for which we heartily thank them.

Chapter

1

Introduction

In recent years, there have been many announcements of new technologies that promise to change the way data is forwarded, or switched, in the Internet and other networks based on the Internet protocol suite. Many of these technologies are based on a set of common ideas. They all use a label swapping technique for forwarding data, the same technique that, not coincidentally, is used to forward data in ATM switches. Unlike ATM, however, all the techniques strive to maintain the control paradigm of the Internet protocol suite. They use IP addresses and standard Internet routing protocols such as OSPF and BGP. Thus in many respects they combine the best of ATM (fast, simple forwarding) with the best of IP (ubiquity, scalability, flexibility). All the approaches enable unmodified ATM switch hardware to be used as a router, given the addition of suitable software. There are also many significant differences between the approaches, such as the use of either data or control traffic to drive the establishment of forwarding state. Also, some of the approaches run only on ATM hardware, whereas some run on a wide variety of platforms including existing routers.

The first approach of this type to gain significant attention in the marketplace (although not the first to be publicly disclosed) was dubbed *IP Switching* by its inventors at the start-up company Ipsilon. Toshiba had previously described a similar scheme, implemented in their *Cell Switching Router* (CSR), and several other approaches were soon published, notably Cisco's *Tag Switching* and IBM's *Aggregate Route-based IP Switching* (ARIS). This book provides a detailed description and analysis of this new set of approaches to forwarding data in internetworks. It explores the problem space and explains the factors that led to such a flurry of activity in this area. It describes the overall architectural issues that are raised and addressed by these approaches and presents several of the proposed schemes in detail, with an exploration of the different design choices that have been made and a discussion of the pros and cons of those choices.

It is important that we define some terms at this early stage. One word that we have already used several times is *forwarding*. We use this to refer to the common operation that both switches and routers perform on packets: they receive a packet on an input, determine where it needs to go by examining some fields in the packet, and send it to the appropriate output.

The set of approaches described in this book will be referred to collectively as *label switching* technologies. A *label* is simply a relatively short, fixed-length identifier that is used to forward packets. Label values are normally local to a single link (more precisely, a single data link layer subnet) and thus have no global significance. They are also unstructured; that is, they are not made up of distinct components. A label switching device will usually replace the label in a packet with some new value before forwarding it on to the next hop. For this reason we call the forwarding algorithm *label swapping*. Forwarding decisions based on labels use the *exact match* algorithm to decide where to send the packets; we describe this algorithm in detail in Chapter 2. And, by our definition, a label switching device, which we will call a *label switching router* (LSR), runs standard IP control protocols (e.g., routing protocols, RSVP, etc.) to determine where to forward packets.

We will examine four approaches in detail in this book. All of them are LSRs by the above definition, and each has its own terminology. The vendor-specific terms for LSRs are *Cell Switching Router (CSR), IP Switch, Tag Switching Router (TSR)* or *Tag Switch*, and *Integrated Switch Router (ISR)*. There are other approaches that we have not covered, either because they did not differ significantly enough from these four to add much to the discussion, or because they were not label switching approaches. In particular, we have not covered *switch-based routers*, which behave externally like a conventional router but which are built internally around a switching fabric. Such devices are interesting pieces of hardware, but address a different set of problems than LSRs. They focus primarily on performance, which is only a small part of the problem space addressed by label switching.

In the later chapters of this book we review the state of the standards in this area, which are being defined by the Internet Engineering Task Force (IETF) at the time of writing. The IETF, looking for a neutral term, has adopted the phrase *Multiprotocol Label Switching* (MPLS) to refer to these techniques. We will use the term *label switching* when speaking generically about the full range of related technologies, and *MPLS* when talking explicitly about the IETF standards.

Before looking at the details of any of these approaches, however, it will be helpful to consider the set of factors that led to the focus of attention in this area.

1.1　How Did We Get Here?

Many factors led to the development of the label switching field. It is often assumed that there was just one factor—the need for fast, cheap IP routers. This may be true for one or two of the approaches, but, as we will see in the following sections, the label switching field as a whole was driven by much more than just the need for speed. In the following discussion, each factor may have been important in the development of only a subset of the label switching approaches. However, it is the combination of all these factors that has caused the field to develop to the point where label switching seems certain to be part of the networking landscape for the foreseeable future.

1.1.1 *Growth and Evolution of the Internet*

It is by now something of a cliché to talk about the "explosive" or "exponential" growth of the Internet, but the fact remains that it has experienced remarkable growth. The Internet is clearly getting bigger in almost any dimension that can be measured, and this growth has created a wealth of technical challenges. Label switching is in part a response to these challenges.

The growth in both the number of users of the Internet and in their bandwidth requirements have placed increasing demands on the Internet service providers' (ISPs) networks. To meet the growing demand for bandwidth, ISPs need higher performance switching and routing products. We discuss the role of performance in motivating the label switching effort in the next section.

As well as getting faster, networks need to deal with increased numbers of nodes, more routes in routing tables, more flows passing through a given point, and so forth. In general, network providers need to be concerned with *scalability*, which we can define loosely as the ability to grow the network in all these dimensions without finding some insurmountable problem. Label switching has been in part motivated by the need for scalability, which we discuss further in Section 1.1.3.

Perhaps the most important motivating factor behind label switching, and certainly one that is not well appreciated in the networking community, is the need to evolve the routing functionality of the Internet and of IP networks in general. The growth of the Internet is continually placing new demands on the routing protocols, and there is an ever-growing need for new routing functionality—both to deal with the growth itself and to meet the evolving needs of the growing user population.

In the past, routing functionality was notoriously difficult to evolve, and part of the reason is the close coupling between routing and forwarding in IP networks. As an example, consider the process of deploying Classless Interdomain Routing (CIDR). The effect of CIDR is to say that IP network prefixes, which had previously been 8, 16, or 24 bits long, could now be of any length. This greatly enhanced the efficiency with which addresses could be assigned in the Internet and also helped enable more scaleable aggregation of addressing and routing information. However, making this change also required a change in the forwarding algorithm of virtually all IP routers, because prefixes could now be of any length. These algorithms are crucial to the performance of a router and are either implemented in hardware or very finely tuned software. Making changes to the forwarding algorithms is typically an expensive and time-consuming proposition.

One of the attractions of label switching is that the forwarding algorithm is fixed and that new control paradigms can be deployed without making any changes to it. As we will see in the next chapter, a wide variety of control modules can be used to control the label switching process, and they all use exactly the same forwarding algorithm. Thus it is entirely feasible to put the forwarding algorithm in hardware or to tune the fast path software once without concern that it will need to be re-optimized every time a new piece of routing functionality is required. This has significant potential to shorten the time it takes to develop and deploy new routing functionality in IP networks. It is our belief that this is the most significant benefit of label switching and that as a result label switching is likely to form the foundation for the next generation of routing architecture.

Some readers may at this point be wondering what happened to IP version 6 (IPv6). Wasn't it supposed to be the basis of the next generation of IP networks? The reality is that IPv6 serves a very specific purpose: extending the IP address space so that a greater number of IP nodes can be uniquely addressed. IPv6 actually makes no change to the routing architecture that was developed for IP version 4 (IPv4). New functionality, such as resource reservations, security, and so on, which are often discussed in the same breath with IPv6, are largely independent of it.

Interestingly, label switching has the potential to simplify the deployment of IPv6, because it would require no change to the forwarding algorithms. All of the label switching techniques described in this book could operate with IPv6, given the availability of routing protocols that carry IPv6 addresses.

1.1.2 *Price and Performance*

In any network based on the Internet protocol suite, whether it is part of the global Internet or a private internetwork,[1] one of the key components is the router. The most fundamental task of a router is to forward IP packets (or datagrams) across the network. As we will see in more detail in the next chapter, forwarding IP datagrams is a rather complex operation. Furthermore, routers often perform a wide range of functions in addition to just forwarding packets, such as filtering the flow of packets between different parts of a network. Indeed the most important characteristic of a router for many applications is not how fast it can forward packets but how rich a set of functionality it provides.

Another important network component is the switch. Whereas routers are layer 3 devices (they forward IP packets, and IP is a layer 3 protocol in the 7-layer protocol model), switches are layer 2 devices—they forward layer 2 protocol packets. Compared to routers, switches tend to be rather simple. They do not provide the same rich set of features, and they normally support a very limited number of protocols and interface types. By contrast, routers usually support dozens of protocols and a wide range of interface types and speeds. The forwarding algorithm of a switch is invariably very simple. Some types of switches, notably ATM switches and frame relay switches, use a forwarding algorithm based on label swapping.

Given the different complexity of the tasks performed by routers and switches, it is not surprising that they tend to exhibit different price/performance characteristics. First, we should define what we mean by performance. Characterizing the performance of a switch or a router can be quite complex because it tends to depend on many factors, such as the exact traffic pattern presented to the inputs of the device. However, it is normally possible to come up with a reasonably representative performance number

---

[1] In this book we follow the convention of using the term *Internet* (spelled with a capital *I*) to refer specifically to the well-known global network with which most readers are familiar, whereas we use the generic term *internetwork* to refer to an arbitrary network based on the Internet protocol suite.

either in terms of the packets per second that the device can forward between inputs and outputs or in terms of its total bandwidth capacity. For example, if a switch has 10 inputs, each of which can accept data at 150 Mbps (150×10^6 bits/second), and it can switch data from all of those inputs simultaneously, we might say it has a total capacity of 1.5 Gbps ($10 \times 150 \times 10^6 = 1.5 \times 10^9$ bits/second).

When we look at the price/performance characteristics of switches and routers, we usually find that switches come out ahead. By this we mean that, for a given performance level, the price of the router tends to be higher than the equivalent switch. Conversely, for a given cost, a switch tends to offer a higher performance level than a router. This is not too surprising when you consider that the router has to forward packets and perform various other services, while the switch, in essence, does very little but forward packets. This performance difference is exacerbated by the fact that the actual forwarding operation of a router is more complex than that of a switch, for reasons discussed in the next chapter.

Related to this observation is the fact that the highest level of performance at any given time has usually been found in switches rather than routers. Thus, for example, switches capable of handling 10 Gbits of total capacity were available well before routers of similar capacity.

There remains considerable room for debate about whether the observed price/performance differences between switches and routers are fundamental or are just historical artifacts resulting from different design goals, marketing strategies, and any number of other factors. However, it is very hard to dispute the observed price/performance differences at the point in time when the various label switching schemes were proposed.

This leads directly to one of the key motivations for the development of all the label switching approaches. What if you could build a device that did the most important job of a router—forwarding IP packets—using hardware that looks like a switch? You would have a product that has the price/performance characteristics of a switch, but the functionality of a router. Of course, you might not get all the more esoteric router features, but in some situations, those features aren't really necessary. This has become even more attractive as the success of the Internet has increased the number of situations in which IP is the only protocol that a router needs to handle. It was the desire to provide IP forwarding at the price/performance level of a switch that motivated much of the work described in this book.

1.1.3 *Integration of IP over ATM*

Another factor motivating much of the work described in this book is the desire to integrate IP and ATM (asynchronous transfer mode). ATM switches started to appear on the market in the late 1980s and promised to provide great performance improvements over earlier network technologies. However, as the standards for ATM networks evolved, driven by bodies such as the International Telecommunications Union (ITU; the primary standards-setting body for telecommunications equipment, formerly known as CCITT) and the ATM Forum, ATM acquired an architectural model that differed significantly from that of the IP protocol suite. Notably, whereas IP is based on a datagram or connectionless model of data delivery, ATM is based on a connection-oriented or virtual circuit model. IP and ATM also have completely separate addressing schemes and a host of other differences, including different models of multicast communication and resource allocation. These different architectural models presented a significant challenge, and the label switching efforts were in part a response to that challenge.

In the early stages of ATM's development, it seemed possible (to some observers, at least) that ATM would "conquer the world," that is, become the dominant networking technology. Many hardcore ATM advocates imagined the development of native ATM-based applications and new protocol stacks designed to take advantage of the features of ATM. However, it soon became apparent that a major function of many ATM networks would be the forwarding of IP datagrams. This was in large part the result of the success of the Internet, and of the fact that TCP/IP-based applications, such as Web browsers, had become entrenched. Thus, the

ATM and IP standards bodies were faced with the problem of how to "map" the IP architecture onto ATM networks.

A factor making this problem even more pressing was the difference in performance between ATM switches and commercially available routers. The relatively high performance of ATM switches, and the fact that ATM had been designed to operate over wide area links, made ATM an attractive technology with which to build the backbone of an internetwork. Some large parts of today's Internet are built out of ATM switches surrounded by relatively low speed routers. An example of such a network design is shown in Figure 1.1.

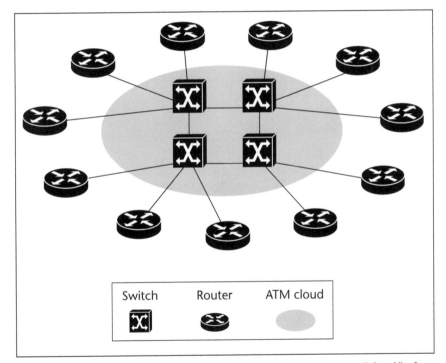

Figure 1.1   *An IP over ATM network. Routers connect to a "cloud" of ATM switches.*

The type of network shown here is often said to use the *overlay model*. The idea is that the IP network is overlaid onto an ATM network. The ATM network provides a core of high speed connectivity, and the IP network, which is composed of a set of routers interconnected by ATM virtual circuits, provides the intelligence to forward IP datagrams, which is the main job of the network.

The problem of mapping IP onto ATM was taken up by a number of standards bodies, primarily the ATM Forum and the IETF. The complexity of the problem can be appreciated to some extent just by counting the number of different working groups that have tackled aspects of this mapping problem. These include

- The IP over ATM (IPATM) working group, which defined encapsulations for IP datagrams when carried inside ATM adaptation layer PDUs and an address resolution protocol (ATMARP) for mapping IP addresses to ATM addresses, which was later extended to handle multicast

- The IP over Large Public Data Networks (IPLPDN) and later Routing over Large Clouds (ROLC) working groups, which defined the Next Hop Resolution Protocol (NHRP) to enable widely separated hosts and routers to establish direct virtual circuits across an ATM network

- The LAN Emulation working group (LANE), which defined procedures to make an ATM network appear to behave more like a multiaccess LAN

- The Multiprotocol over ATM (MPOA) working group, which combined and extended the work of many of the other groups to support multiple network layer protocols (as opposed to just IP)

- The Integrated Services over Specific Link Layers (ISSLL) working group, which is defining procedures to map the resource reservation model of IP onto that of ATM (along with other link layers)

As this quick survey suggests, mapping between IP and ATM involves considerable complexity. Most of the above groups have defined some sort of server (ATMARP, MARS, NHRP, BUS, to name a few) to handle one of the mapping functions, along with the protocols necessary to interact with the server. A continuing problem is dealing with the fact that servers represent a single point of failure, and thus there is a desire to make redundant servers, which of course require synchronization protocols to keep them consistent with each other.

Where did all this complexity come from? In essence, it all derives from the fact that the Internet protocols and the ATM protocols were developed with virtually no regard for each other and happened to end up in very different places. This realization has prompted a lot of people to wonder if ATM switches could be used with a different set of protocols than those defined by the ATM Forum and the ITU—a set of protocols that are more consistent with the Internet architecture and that would eliminate the need for the plethora of complex mappings. Several label switching efforts described in this book are in fact attempts to define such a set of protocols, which can control an ATM switch in such a way that it naturally forwards IP packets without the help of half a dozen servers mapping between IP and ATM.

As we will see in the following chapters, the various schemes to forward IP packets using label switching all do away with the overlay model and the complexity it brings. Instead of having two different protocol architectures with different addressing, routing protocols, resource allocations schemes, and so on, all of the proposals enable IP control protocols to run directly on ATM hardware. The ATM switches still forward packets using label swapping, but the mechanisms by which they set up the forwarding tables and allocate resources are all driven by IP control protocols. From a control point of view, the ATM switches effectively *become* IP routers, thus removing the need to map between IP and ATM control models.

Scalability Issues

There is a little-known but important scaling problem that arises whenever an IP network is built as an overlay on a layer 2 mesh, as might be done with a frame relay backbone as well as an ATM one. By "scaling problem," we mean that some measure of complexity in the network grows much faster than the number of nodes in the network, so that at some point it just becomes unfeasible to make the network any bigger.

Consider the network in Figure 1.1. If the ATM network in the middle is to provide high speed connectivity among all the routers, a full mesh of virtual circuits (VCs) must interconnect all the routers. Anything less would mean that there would be an extra router hop between some pairs of routers, which could cause the extra router in the middle of the path to become a bottleneck. However, a full mesh of VCs means that all the routers are, in effect, directly connected to each other. In Figure 1.2, to avoid cluttering the diagram, we have shown only the VCs that originate at one of the routers; in reality, a full mesh would consist of $n(n - 1)/2$ VCs, or 55 VCs, in this example.

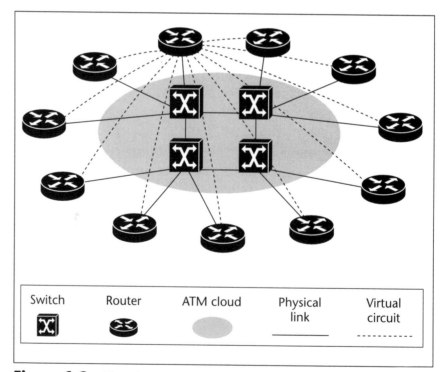

Switch	Router	ATM cloud	Physical link	Virtual circuit

Figure 1.2 *Virtual circuits between routers over an ATM network.*

To appreciate the problem here, it is necessary to know a little about how routing protocols work. A router is normally configured to have an *adjacency* with each of its directly connected neighbors. The adjacencies enable the router to keep track of who it is directly connected to and whether any links have gone down and are used to exchange routing information with those neighbors.

When the routers are connected by a full mesh of virtual circuits, the number of immediate neighbors any router has is equal to the number of routers around the cloud minus one (itself). The fact that there are ATM switches between the routers doesn't prevent them from appearing to be directly connected at the network layer—the switches are effectively invisible at this layer. So, in Figure 1.2, the number of adjacencies any router has is 10—the number of other routers connected to the cloud. Thus, the lines in the figure represent not only VCs but also routing adjacencies.

It can be shown that the amount of routing information that is transmitted in such a network in the presence of a topology change in the core of the network can be as much as the order of n^4, where n is the number of routers around the core. (The derivation of this result is too involved to present here.) Because the amount of information grows so quickly with increasing n, it can reach a point where routing traffic alone can overload a router, leading to very poor performance. Thus we conclude that such a design is poor from a scaling perspective.

Several approaches can be taken to alleviate this scaling problem. One place to start is to eliminate the full mesh of VCs. As we observed, this means that the path between some pairs of routers will now involve an extra router hop, which may be acceptable if the performance of the intermediate router is adequate to handle the extra traffic. Alternatively, the Next Hop Resolution Protocol (NHRP) allows routers to establish VCs over which they can send data without needing to establish a routing adjacency over the VC. This approach has its own set of problems, including the need to run a number of NHRP servers and the possibility of introducing persistent forwarding loops. NHRP is also suitable only for unicast traffic; it is not defined for multicast.

Another approach to solve this scaling problem involves label switching. First, recall that an LSR by definition runs IP control protocols, including IP routing protocols, and may be implemented using unmodified ATM hardware. Thus, without changing the physical topology or devices in Figure 1.2, we can dramatically reduce the number of adjacencies that any one router has by running IP routing protocols on the ATM switches. This is illustrated in Figure 1.3.

Because the ATM switches are able to run IP routing protocols, the notion of an immediate neighbor has now changed from the router on the other end of a VC to the device—router or LSR—at the other end of a physical link. Thus the maximum number of adjacencies that any one router has is greatly reduced and no longer grows with the size of the network, which results in a much more scalable design. Note that the router that had ten adjacencies in Figure 1.2 now has only one and that the LSRs (which used to be ATM switches) have no more than five adjacencies each— one with each directly connected router, whether it is a conventional router or an ATM switch functioning as an LSR.

This is not the only situation in which scalability can be improved with label switching. We consider another situation that is not specific to ATM in Section 5.1.2.

1.1.4 *Extending Routing Functionality*

It is important to emphasize that label switching is not just about making ATM hardware behave more like an IP router. Nor is it just about making faster, cheaper IP routers. Label switching also enables new functionality that could not readily be provided with existing IP routing techniques. The ability to offer new routing capabilities has been another motivating factor behind the development of some (although not all) label switching techniques. In this section we are discussing something slightly different from the routing evolution described in Section 1.1.1. The issue here is that label switching enables routing capabilities that conventional routing is unable to support.

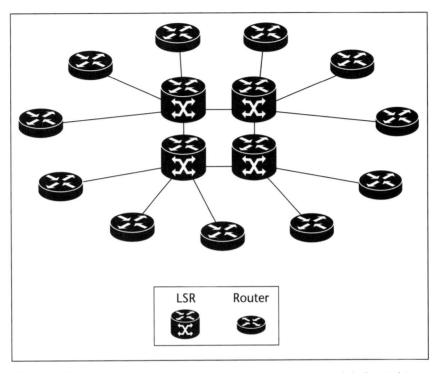

Figure 1.3   *Eliminating a full mesh of adjacencies using label switching. Each router or LSR has an adjacency with its immediate neighbor. Unlike Figure 1.2, in this figure there is just one adjacency on each physical link.*

The most notable example of an area where label switching promises to expand the capabilities of conventional IP routing is the area of destination-based routing. Virtually all routing today in IP networks is destination-based; that is, the decision about where to forward a packet is made based only on its destination address. In principle, other fields in the IP header (e.g., source address, type of service bits) could be used when deciding where to forward a packet, but various design considerations have led to router designs that almost always forward based on destination address alone. By contrast, network technologies that rely on label swapping techniques, such as frame relay and ATM, can provide different functionality.

To understand how label switching enables new functionality, consider the network shown in Figure 1.4. This is a classic example of a type of function that is hard to provide with conventional routing. It is sometimes called "the fish picture" because the network resembles a fish in profile. Consider the case where router B is a conventional router that forwards packets using only the IP destination address. When a packet arrives at B from one of its neighbors, the forwarding decision is not affected by any factor other than destination address. Now suppose we wanted router B to implement the simple policy "packets arriving from A that are going to router F should go via router D, while all other packets destined for F should go via router E." A forwarding mechanism that looks only at destination clearly cannot implement this policy.

By contrast, it is rather easy to implement such a policy at B if B forwards packets based on label switching. The main reason is that A and C are under no obligation to use the same label for all packets going to router F. Suppose A uses a label value of 5 for packets destined for F, while C uses the label value 12. Thus, when the packets arrive at router B, it can forward packets with label 5 to router D and packets with label 12 to router E.

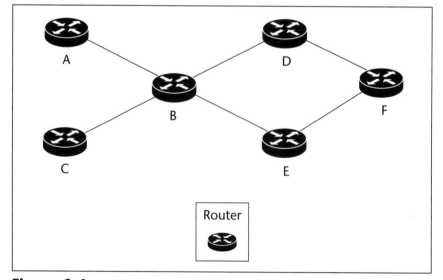

Figure 1.4   *Label switched paths.*

Although this brief example glosses over the details, it should be clear that label switching enables new routing functionality to be deployed in devices that are also able to function as IP routers. We will look much more closely at how label switching enables new types of routing functionality in Chapter 2.

1.2 A Brief History

Now that we have seen some of the reasons why the inventors of the various approaches to label switching felt the need to invent them, it is worth taking a brief look at the sequence of events that led up to the current situation. As we noted in the previous section, label switching tries to solve a wider range of problems than just the integration of IP and ATM; nevertheless, it is fair to say that the problems that existed in mapping between the protocol models of IP and ATM were significant drivers in the development of label switching. Thus, we start our historical overview by briefly reviewing the IP over ATM situation prior to the arrival of the first label switching techniques. We will look more closely at IP over ATM in Chapter 3.

1.2.1 *IP over ATM*

Attempts to standardize ATM protocols have been going on since the 1980s, and a need was soon recognized in the IP community (at least the part of it that wasn't just hoping ATM would go away) to figure out how to carry IP datagrams over ATM networks. A number of IETF working groups tackled this problem, and two notable Requests for Comments (RFCs)[2] were produced in 1993 and 1994.

The first IP over ATM standard, described in RFC 1483, addresses the apparently simple problem of how to encapsulate IP datagrams (and packets of other protocols) on an ATM link. The second, RFC 1577, defines "classical IP over ATM" and ATMARP.

---

[2] The RFC series is a collection of documents archived by the IETF, almost all of which are kept online, and which include all Internet standards. However, by no means are all RFCs standards; some have even been April Fools' jokes.

The classical model assumes that ATM networks are used much like other subnet technologies, which means that IP routers and hosts can communicate over a subnet if they are on the same subnet, that is, if the network and subnet parts of their addresses are the same. If they are on different subnets, then one or more routers need to be involved to forward the packet from the source subnet to the sink subnet.

In defining the classical IP over ATM model, it was recognized that IP devices could be connected to a common ATM network (e.g., a large ATM network offered by a public carrier) yet be on different subnets. Thus the idea of a logical IP subnet (LIS) was introduced. A LIS consists of the set of IP hosts and routers that are connected to a common ATM network and that share a common IP network and subnet address. RFC 1577 only addresses communication within a LIS and assumes that to get a packet from one LIS to another, it needs to go through a router that is connected to both LISs. This is illustrated in Figure 1.5.

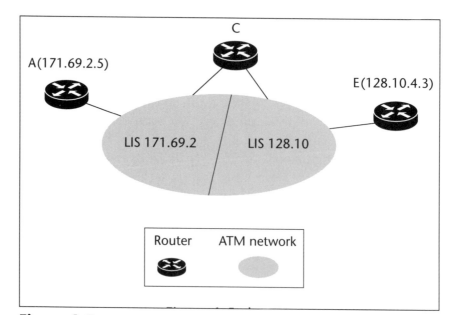

Figure 1.5 *Logical IP subnets. A single ATM network is divided into two logical IP subnets. Routers A and E are on different LISs and so must communicate through router C in the classical model.*

The first thing to notice about the classical model is that it implies that two IP devices connected to the same ATM network but on separate LISs will not be able to use a single VC across the ATM network to send IP datagrams to each other. Instead, they need to send packets through a router. This approach seemed unattractive to many people, especially given the high performance of commercially available ATM switches relative to routers at the time of this work. Although it might appear that this problem could be solved by decreeing that the ATM network must be a single LIS, this is often difficult for administrative reasons. For example, two unrelated organizations connected to a single public ATM network are unlikely to want to administer their IP addresses from a common subnet address space.

Having defined the concept of the LIS, RFC 1577 defines the key mechanism needed for two IP devices on the same LIS to establish communication: ATMARP. The Address Resolution Protocol (ARP) is used on conventional media (such as Ethernet) to enable IP devices to learn the address information needed to communicate, for example, the Ethernet address. Similarly, ATMARP allows two IP devices to learn each other's ATM addresses. Because conventional ARP depends on link-layer broadcast, which ATM does not support, ATMARP introduced the concept of an ARP server, a single node on a LIS that provides IP-address-to-ATM-address resolution for the LIS. Each IP device on a LIS registers with the ARP server and provides its ATM address and its IP address. Any device on the LIS can then ask the ARP server to resolve an IP address to an ATM address. Equipped with the ATM address, the device can then set up a virtual circuit to that address using ATM signaling, and then send data.

The problem of establishing an ATM virtual circuit to an IP device on a different LIS, which RFC 1577 does not address, was taken up by the Routing over Large Clouds (ROLC) group of the IETF. The proposed approach to solving the "extra router hop" problem described above was the Next Hop Resolution Protocol (NHRP). NHRP enables an IP device on one logical IP subnet to learn the ATM address of another IP device on a different subnet through the use of one or more "next hop servers." The details of this protocol are rather complex and not strictly relevant to this discussion; it is sufficient to note here that, as with ATMARP, NHRP enables an IP device to learn the ATM address of another IP device with which it wants to communicate, and thus it can set up an ATM VC to that device using ATM signaling.

1.2.2 Toshiba's Cell Switching Router (CSR)

All of the work just described makes the basic assumption that routers do routing and ATM switches do ATM switching and never the twain shall meet. The work embodied in Toshiba's CSR proposal represents one of the first publicly described pieces of work that called that assumption into question. The CSR architecture, which we explore in detail in Chapter 3, introduced the idea that an ATM switching fabric could be controlled by IP protocols (such as IP routing and RSVP) rather than ATM signalling protocols such as Q.2931. Such an approach, if carried to its logical conclusion, could do away with the need for virtually all ATM signaling and all the mapping functions between IP and ATM. Also, as the CSR proponents noted, a mixture of conventional ATM switches and CSRs could be used; for example, CSRs could interconnect LISs to remove the need for NHRP.

The CSR ideas were presented first to an IETF working group meeting and later at a "Birds of a Feather" (BOF)[3] session of the IETF in 1994 and early 1995. It is probably fair to assume that many other organizations were developing similar ideas at the time. However, the BOF did not result in a clear definition of a problem that the IETF needed to address, and the level of public activity in the field remained fairly low.

---

[3] Birds of a Feather sessions are the necessary precursor to forming a working group. They are held to determine whether there is a problem that needs a standards-based solution and to establish the level of interest in the IETF community. Not all BOFs lead to working groups.

1.2.3 *IP Switching*

For a variety of reasons including more complete technical specifications, better timing, the existence of a production quality product (as opposed to a prototype), and effective marketing, IP Switching, as defined by the start-up company Ipsilon, made a much larger impact in the marketplace and the trade press than the CSR approach. Ipsilon announced their approach in early 1996. Technically, the two approaches have considerable similarities, as we will see in the detailed discussion of each of them in subsequent chapters. However, the advantages of IP Switching over other well-known approaches can be clearly stated and understood:

- ■ IP Switching enables a device with the performance of an ATM switch to perform the job of a router.

- ■ Fast routers (not ATM switches) are what's needed today because IP, the protocol of the Internet, is the dominant protocol and existing routers are too slow.

- ■ ATM signaling and mapping IP to ATM has become so complex that, for the purposes of IP forwarding, we're better off without ATM control protocols altogether.

These arguments are in fact brief versions of some of the motivations described in Section 1.1 for the whole label switching effort. Many people found them very compelling.

Ipsilon documented their approach in a number of informational Internet RFCs. As already noted, not all RFCs are standards (informational RFCs are not), but this nevertheless enabled Ipsilon to legitimately claim that theirs was an "open" approach because the basic protocols were publicly available. Another significant contribution was the specification of a simple switch control protocol (GSMP) that could enable virtually any ATM switch be turned into an "IP switch" with the addition of an external controller.

For the sake of clarity, we will use the term *IP Switching* to refer specifically to the Ipsilon approach, even though it is often used elsewhere to refer to a wider range of approaches. When a generic term is needed, we will use the term *label switching*.

1.2.4 *Tag Switching*

A few months after Ipsilon's announcement, Cisco Systems announced another approach to label switching, which they named *Tag Switching*. As we will see in the following chapters, Tag Switching was a significant technical departure from IP Switching and the CSR approach. For example, it did not rely on the flow of data traffic to set up forwarding tables in the switch, and it was specified for a number of link layer technologies other than ATM.

Like Ipsilon, Cisco produced an informational RFC describing the approach. Unlike Ipsilon, however, Cisco announced its intention to pursue the standardization of Tag Switching through the IETF. In this vein, a large number of Internet drafts were produced, describing many aspects of Tag Switching, including operation over ATM, PPP and 802.3 links, support for multicast routing, and support for resource reservation using RSVP. The standardization effort that Cisco started became known as the Multiprotocol Label Switching (MPLS) working group, the history of which is described in Section 1.2.6.

1.2.5 *IBM's ARIS*

Shortly after Cisco's announcement of Tag Switching and the effort to standardize it in the IETF, a number of Internet drafts were submitted by authors from IBM describing another label switching approach called *Aggregate Route-based IP Switching*, or *ARIS*. As we will see in later chapters, ARIS has more in common with Tag Switching than with the other approaches mentioned so far—both use control traffic rather than data traffic to set up forwarding tables—but ARIS also differs from Tag Switching in some significant ways.

1.2.6 *The Multiprotocol Label Switching (MPLS) Working Group*

When Cisco made its announcement about Tag Switching, it also announced its intention to standardize the technology. Following the publication of the first set of Tag Switching Internet drafts, a BOF session was held in December 1996, with presentations made by Cisco, IBM, and Toshiba (who had, by this time, produced a new set of Internet drafts on the CSR approach). The BOF session was one of the most well attended in IETF history.

The level of interest in the BOF, and the fact that so many companies had produced fairly similar proposals to solve a problem, made it clear that a standardization effort was in order. Even though some doubt existed as to whether the problem being solved was an important one (e.g., some people made the argument that faster routers would make the whole problem irrelevant), there was no doubt that, without a standards group, there would be a proliferation of incompatible label switching techniques. Thus, an effort to charter a working group began, and a charter was successfully accepted by the IETF in early 1997. The first meeting of the working group was held in April 1997.

As noted above, the name *Multiprotocol Label Switching* was adopted primarily because the names *IP Switching* and *Tag Switching* were each associated with the products of a single company, and a vendor-neutral term was required. In spite of the decision to use the word *multiprotocol* in the name, there has been little interest so far in considering any network layer protocol other than IP.

At the time of writing (January 1998), the working group has made considerable progress, the details of which are described in Chapter 8. However, Cisco, Toshiba, and Ipsilon all have products based on their own approaches that predate the standard, so it is important to examine the details of each approach. This we will do in the following chapters.

1.3 Summary

The label switching area, which includes various flavors of IP Switching, Tag Switching, and Multiprotocol Label Switching (MPLS), has become a focus of great attention. This area has become important as designers seek to solve several related problems:

- The need to evolve the routing architecture of IP networks
- The need for greater performance, or better price/performance characteristics, in routers
- The seemingly ever-increasing complexity of mapping IP to ATM
- Scalability
- The need to add new routing functionality

There has been a tendency to view label switching as only addressing one or two of these areas and thus to underestimate its impact. Although other solutions that address some of these areas may appear, we believe that the ability of label switching to address all of them makes it likely that label switching will provide a foundation for the next generation of routing architecture.

A wide variety of techniques have been proposed to address the above problems. All the techniques use label swapping as the forwarding algorithm, and all run IP control protocols. Consequently, any of the approaches can turn an ATM switch into a device that behaves exactly like a router from a control point of view. It is not, however, required to use ATM hardware to build a label switching router. For example, a standard software-based router can also implement label switching.

There are many important differences between the various label switching techniques, the details of which will be the focus of most of the rest of the book. In particular, the various approaches have different contributions to make in addressing problems of scalability and routing evolution. The IETF label switching standard, MPLS, should combine the best of the existing approaches and thus provide a solution that will have a significant impact on networks of the future.

Further Reading

We will provide references to publications describing each of the label switching approaches at the end of each chapter. For this chapter, we provide references to the IP over ATM standards that preceded and to some extent motivated label switching.

The standards for classical IP over ATM are

Heinanen, J. *Multiprotocol Encapsulation over AAL5*. RFC 1483, July 1993.

Laubach, M. *Classical IP and ARP over ATM*. RFC 1577, January 1994.

Like all RFCs, they can be found at

ftp://ds.internic.net/rfc

The Next Hop Resolution Protocol has not made it to RFC status at the time of writing but is expected to do so soon and then will be found in the same place as the above references. The latest Internet drafts on NHRP (or any other subject) can be found via the IETF Web page at

www.ietf.org/1id-abstracts.html

Further information on IP addressing, routing, and forwarding can be found in any number of introductory texts, such as

Comer, D. E. *Internetworking with TCP/IP. Vol. 1: Principles, Protocols, and Architecture*. 3rd ed. Englewood Cliffs, NJ: Prentice-Hall, 1995.

Peterson, L., and B. Davie. *Computer Networks: A Systems Approach*. San Francisco: Morgan Kaufmann, 1996.

Chapter

2

Fundamental Concepts

In this section we describe the fundamental concepts of label switching. Although there are differences among various approaches to label switching, certain concepts are common to all of these approaches—such concepts form the fundamental building blocks of label switching. A solid grasp of these concepts will help you understand the individual approaches to label switching as well as to compare them.

We begin this chapter with a description of the functional decomposition of network layer routing into control and forwarding components. We then proceed to describe label switching forwarding and control components. While describing the label switching control component, we present and compare various design alternatives. We then describe the type of devices that are needed to support label switching, followed by a brief discussion of the relationship between label switching and network layer routing and addressing. The chapter concludes with a brief summary.

2.1 Network Layer Routing Functional Components: Control and Forwarding

Network layer routing can be partitioned into two basic components: control and forwarding. The forwarding component is responsible for the actual forwarding of packets from input to output across a switch or router. To forward a packet the forwarding component uses two sources of information: a forwarding table maintained by a router and the information carried in the packet itself. The control component is responsible for construction and maintenance of the forwarding table.

Each router in a network implements both control and forwarding components. The actual network layer routing is realized as a composition of control and forwarding components implemented in a distributed fashion by a set of routers that forms the network.

The control component consists of one or more routing protocols that provide exchange of routing information among routers, as well as the procedures (algorithms) that a router uses to convert this information into a forwarding table. OSPF, BGP, and PIM are examples of such routing protocols.

The forwarding component consists of a set of procedures (algorithms) that a router uses to make a forwarding decision on a packet. The algorithms define the information from the packet that a router uses to find a particular entry in its forwarding table, as well as the exact procedures that the router uses for finding the entry. As an illustration, we consider three cases: (1) forwarding of unicast packets, (2) forwarding of unicast packets with Types of Service, and (3) forwarding of multicast packets.

For unicast forwarding, the information from a packet that a router uses to find a particular entry in the forwarding table is the network layer destination address, and the procedure that the router uses for finding the entry is the longest match algorithm.

For unicast forwarding with Types of Service, the information from a packet that a router uses to find a particular entry in the forwarding table is the network layer destination address and the Type of Service value, and the procedure that the router uses for finding the entry is the longest match algorithm on the destination address and the exact match algorithm on the Type of Service value.

For multicast forwarding, the information from a packet that a router uses to find a particular entry in the forwarding table is a combination of the network layer source and destination addresses and the incoming interface (the interface that a packet arrives on), and the procedure that the router uses for finding the entry uses both the longest and the exact match algorithms.

2.1.1 *Forwarding Equivalence Classes*

We may think about procedures used by the forwarding component as a way of partitioning the set of all possible packets that a router can forward into a finite number of disjoint subsets. From a forwarding point of view, packets within each subset are treated by the router in the same way (e.g., they are all sent to the same next hop), even if the packets within the subset differ from each other with respect to the information in the network layer header of these packets. We refer to such subsets as Forwarding Equivalence Classes (FECs). The reason a router forwards all packets within a given FEC the same way is that the mapping between the information carried in the network layer header of the packets and the entries in the forwarding table is many-to-one (with one-to-one as a special case). That is, packets with different network layer headers could be mapped into the same entry in the forwarding table, where the entry describes a particular FEC.

One example of an FEC is a set of unicast packets whose destination address matches a particular IP address prefix. A set of multicast packets with the same source and destination network layer addresses is another example of an FEC. A set of unicast packets whose destination addresses match a particular IP address prefix and whose Type of Service bits are the same is yet another example of an FEC.

An essential part of a forwarding entry maintained by a router is the address of the next hop router. A packet that falls into an FEC associated with a particular forwarding entry is forwarded to the next hop router specified by the entry. Therefore, the construction of a forwarding table by the control component means constructing a set of FECs and the next hop for each of these FECs.

One important characteristic of an FEC is its forwarding granularity. For example, at one end of the spectrum, an FEC could include all the packets whose network layer destination address matches a particular address prefix. This type of FEC provides coarse forwarding granularity. At the other end of the spectrum, an FEC could include only the packets that belong to a particular application running between a pair of computers, thus including only the packets with the same source and destination network layer addresses (these addresses identify the computers), as well as the transport layer port numbers (these ports identify a particular application within a computer). This type of FEC provides fine forwarding granularity.

One could observe that coarse forwarding granularity is essential for making the overall system scaleable. On the other hand, supporting only coarse granularity would make the overall system fairly inflexible, as it wouldn't allow differentiation among different types of traffic. For example, it would not allow different forwarding or resource reservations for traffic that belongs to different applications. These observations suggest that to build a routing system that is both scaleable and functionally rich would require the system to support a wide spectrum of forwarding granularities, as well as the ability to flexibly intermix and combine different forwarding granularities.

2.1.2 *Providing Consistent Routing*

A correctly functioning routing system requires consistent forwarding across multiple routers. This consistency is accomplished via a combination of several mechanisms.

The control component is responsible for consistent distribution of routing information used by the routers for constructing their forwarding tables. The control component is also responsible for the consistency of the procedures that the routers use to construct their forwarding tables (and thus FECs and associated next hops) out of the routing information. Combining these two factors—consistent information distribution and consistent local procedures—results in consistency among forwarding tables, and therefore FECs and associated next hops, across routers that form a network.

The forwarding component is responsible for consistent procedures for extracting the information from packets, as well as for a consistent way of using this information to find an appropriate entry in a forwarding table, resulting in a consistent mapping of packets into FECs across multiple routers. Consistent mapping of packets into FECs, combined with the consistent forwarding tables across multiple routers, provides a correctly functioning routing system.

As an illustration consider an example of unicast forwarding with OSPF as a routing protocol. The OSPF procedures guarantee (by means of reliable flooding) that the link-state information is consistent among a set of routers. The OSPF procedures also guarantee that all these routers will use the same procedure (the Shortest-Path First algorithm) for computing their forwarding tables based on the link-state information. Combining these two factors results in consistent forwarding tables (consistent set of FECs and their next hops) among the routers. The forwarding component guarantees that the only information carried in the packets that will be used for making the forwarding decision will be the destination network layer address and that all the routers will use the longest match algorithm to find an appropriate entry in their forwarding tables.

2.2 Label Switching: The Forwarding Component

Decomposition of network layer routing into control and forwarding components could be applied not only to the "conventional" routing architecture, but to the label switching approach as well. In this section we describe some of the fundamental concepts associated with the label switching forwarding component.

The algorithm used by the label switching forwarding component to make a forwarding decision on a packet uses two sources of information: the first one is a forwarding table maintained by a label switching router (LSR), and the second is a label carried in the packet.

2.2.1 What Is a Label?

A label is a short, fixed-length entity, with no internal structure. A label does not directly encode any of the information from the network layer header. For example, a label does not directly encode network layer addresses (neither source nor destination addresses). The semantics of a label is discussed in Section 2.2.4.

2.2.2 Label Switching Forwarding Tables

Conceptually a forwarding table maintained by an LSR consists of a sequence of entries, where each entry consists of an incoming label, and one or more subentries, where each subentry consists of an outgoing label, an outgoing interface, and the next hop address (see Figure 2.1). Different subentries within an individual entry may have either the same or different outgoing labels. There may be more than one subentry in order to handle multicast forwarding, where a packet that arrives on one interface would need to be sent out on multiple outgoing interfaces.

The forwarding table is indexed by the value contained in the incoming label. That is, the value contained in the incoming label component of the Nth entry in the table is N.

Incoming label	First subentry	Second subentry
Incoming label	Outgoing label Outgoing interface Next hop address	Outgoing label Outgoing interface Next hop address

Figure 2.1 *Forwarding table entry.*

In addition to the information that controls where a packet is forwarded (next hop), an entry in the forwarding table may include the information related to what resources the packet may use, such as a particular outgoing queue that the packet should be placed on.

An LSR could maintain either a single forwarding table, or a forwarding table per each of its interfaces. With the latter option, handling of a packet is determined not just by the label carried in the packet, but also by the interface that the packet arrives on. With the former option, handling of a packet is determined solely by the label carried in the packet. An LSR may use either the first or the second option, or a combination of both.

2.2.3 *Carrying a Label in a Packet*

Essential to the label switching forwarding component is the ability to carry a label in a packet. This can be accomplished in several ways.

Certain link layer technologies, most notably ATM and Frame Relay, can carry a label as part of their link layer header. Specifically, with ATM the label could be carried in either VCI or VPI fields of the ATM header. Likewise, with Frame Relay the label could be carried in the DLCI field of the Frame Relay header.

Using the option of carrying the label as part of the link layer header allows support of label switching with some but not all link layer technologies. Constraining label switching to only the link layer technologies that could carry the label as part of their link layer header would severely limit the usefulness of label switching (as it would immediately exclude the use of label switching over such media as Ethernet or point-to-point links).

A way to support label switching over link layer technologies where the link layer header can't be used to carry a label, is to carry the label in a small "shim" label header. This shim label header is inserted between the link layer and the network layer headers (see Figure 2.2) and thus could be used with any link layer technology. Use of the shim label header allows support of label switching over such link layer technologies as Ethernet, FDDI, Token Ring, point-to-point links, and so on.

2.2.4 *Label Switching Forwarding Algorithm*

The forwarding algorithm used by the forwarding component of label switching is based on label swapping. The algorithm works as follows. When an LSR receives a packet, the router extracts the label from the packet and uses it as an index in its forwarding table. Once the entry indexed by the label is found (this entry has its incoming label component equal to the label extracted from the packet), for each subentry of the found entry the router replaces the label in the packet with the outgoing label from the subentry and sends the packet over the outgoing interface specified by this subentry to the next hop specified by this subentry. If the entry specifies a particular outgoing queue, the router places the packet on the specified queue.

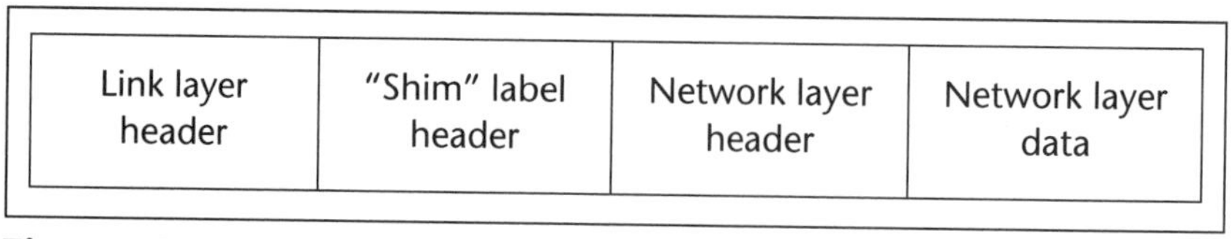

Link layer header	"Shim" label header	Network layer header	Network layer data

Figure 2.2   *Carrying label in the shim label header.*

In the previous paragraph, our description assumes that an LSR maintains a single forwarding table. However, an LSR may also maintain a distinct forwarding table for each of its interfaces. In this case, the only modification to the algorithm is that after the LSR receives a packet, the LSR uses the interface on which the packet was received to select a particular forwarding table that will be used for handling the packet.

Because a label carried in a packet uniquely determines a particular entry in the forwarding table maintained by an LSR, and because that particular entry contains information about where to forward a packet as well as what local resources (e.g., outgoing queue) the packet may use, we could say that the label determines both where the packet will be forwarded, as well as what local resources the packet can use. That is, the label carries both forwarding and resource reservation semantics.

Simplicity of the forwarding algorithm used by the label switching forwarding component facilitates inexpensive implementations of this algorithm in hardware, which, in turn, enables faster forwarding performance without requiring expensive hardware.

One important property of the forwarding algorithm used by label switching is that an LSR can obtain all the information needed to forward a packet, as well as to decide what resources the packet may use in just one memory access. This is because (a) an entry in the forwarding table contains all the information needed to forward a packet, as well as to decide what resources the packet may use, and (b) the label carried in the packet provides an index to the entry in the forwarding table that should be used for forwarding the packet. The ability to obtain both forwarding and resource reservation information in just one memory access makes label switching suitable as a technology for high forwarding performance.

Readers familiar with ATM will notice that when an LSR maintains its forwarding tables on a per-interface basis, the forwarding algorithm just described corresponds to the algorithm used to forward cells in ATM switches. This fact is key to some (but not all) of the label switching approaches we will discuss in the following chapters.

It is important to understand that the use of label swapping forwarding combined with the ability to carry labels on a wide range of link layer technologies means that many different devices can be used to implement LSRs. For example, carrying the label inside the VCI field of ATM cells enables unmodified ATM switch hardware to function as an LSR, given the addition of suitable control software. Similarly, the shim header described above appears in packets in a place where most conventional routers can process it in software. Thus, with the addition of suitable software, a conventional router can also become an LSR. We observe that all the approaches in this book have been defined to work on ATM links and can thus be implemented on ATM hardware. Only a subset are also defined for other media.

2.2.5 *Single Forwarding Algorithm*

In the "conventional" routing architecture, different functionality provided by the control component (e.g., unicast routing, multicast routing, unicast routing with Types of Services) requires multiple forwarding algorithms in the forwarding component (see Figure 2.3). For example, forwarding of unicast packets requires longest match based on the network layer destination address; forwarding of multicast packets requires longest match on the source network layer address plus the exact match on both source and destination network layer addresses, whereas unicast forwarding with Types of Services requires the longest match on the destination network layer address plus the exact match on the Type of Service bits carried in the network layer header.

One important property of label switching is the lack of multiple forwarding algorithms within its forwarding component; the label switching forwarding component consists of just one algorithm—the algorithm based on label swapping (see Figure 2.4). This forms one important distinction between label switching and the conventional routing architecture.

Routing function	Unicast routing	Unicast routing with Types of Services	Multicast routing
Forwarding algorithm	Longest match on destination address	Longest match on destination + exact match on Type of Service	Longest match on source address + exact match on source address, destination address, and incoming interface

Figure 2.3 *Conventional routing architecture.*

Routing function	Unicast routing	Unicast routing with Types of Services	Multicast routing
Forwarding algorithm	Common forwarding (label swapping)		

Figure 2.4 *Label switching architecture.*

One may think that constraining the forwarding component to a single forwarding algorithm would significantly limit the functionality that could be supported with label switching. However, as we will see in later chapters, this is not the case. The ability to support a wide range of routing functionality with just one forwarding algorithm is one of the key assumptions behind label switching, and so far this assumption has proven to be correct. In fact, as we'll see later, the functionality that could be supported with label switching (using a single forwarding algorithm) could be richer than the functionality that could be accomplished with the conventional routing architecture (which uses multiple forwarding algorithms).

2.2.6 *Forwarding Granularity*

The label switching forwarding component, by itself, doesn't place any constraints on the forwarding granularity that could be associated with a particular FEC, and therefore with a label. The spectrum of forwarding granularities that could be associated with FECs, and therefore with labels, as well as the ability to intermix different forwarding granularities, is determined solely by the label switching control component. It is completely up to the control component to decide whether and how to exploit this.

2.2.7 *Multiprotocol: Both Above and Below*

From the previous description of the label switching forwarding component we can make two important observations. First of all, the forwarding component is not specific to a particular network layer. For example, the same forwarding component could be used when doing label switching with IP as well as when doing label switching with IPX. This makes label switching suitable as a multiprotocol solution with respect to the network layer protocols (see Figure 2.5).

Moreover, multiprotocol capabilities of label switching go beyond the ability to support multiple network layer protocols; label switching is also capable of operating over virtually any link layer protocols. This makes label switching a multiprotocol solution with respect to the link layer protocols.

These properties of label switching explain the name given to the IETF working group that is currently working to standardize this technology: Multiprotocol Label Switching (MPLS).

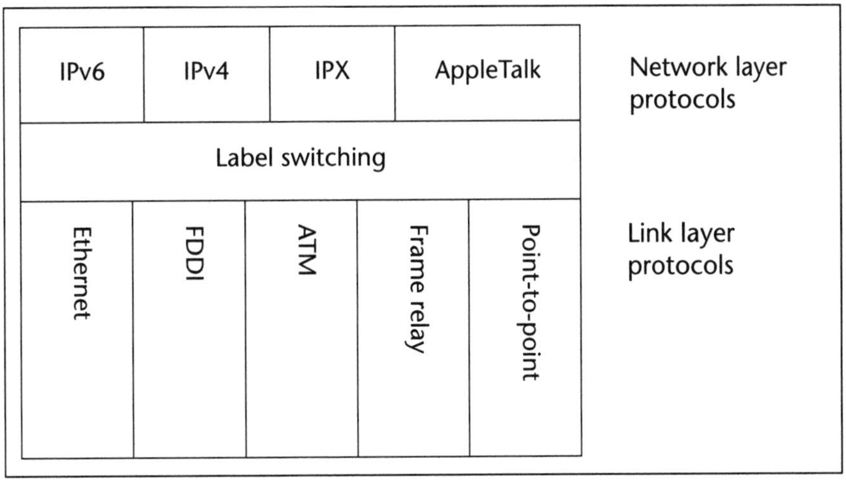

IPv6	IPv4	IPX	AppleTalk	Network layer protocols
Label switching				
Ethernet	FDDI	ATM	Frame relay	Point-to-point	Link layer protocols

Figure 2.5   *Multiprotocol: above and below.*

2.2.8 *Label Switching Forwarding Component: Summary*

As we discussed at the beginning of this section, the forwarding component of network layer routing defines (a) the information from a packet that a router uses for finding a particular entry in its forwarding table, as well as (b) the exact procedures that a router uses for finding the entry. The label switching forwarding component defines a label carried in a packet as the information that an LSR uses to find a particular entry in its forwarding table. The label switching forwarding component defines the exact match on the label as the procedure for finding an entry in a forwarding table.

The following summarizes the rest of the key properties of the label switching forwarding component:

- The label switching forwarding component uses a single forwarding algorithm based on label swapping.
- The label carried in a packet is a short, fixed-length unstructured entity that has both forwarding and resource reservation semantics.

- The label switching forwarding component by itself doesn't place any constraints on the forwarding granularity that could be associated with a label.

- The label switching forwarding component can support multiple network layer protocols as well as multiple link layer protocols.

2.3 Label Switching: The Control Component

As we mentioned before, decomposition of network layer routing into control and forwarding components could be applied not only to the conventional routing architecture, but to label switching as well. In this section we describe some of the fundamental concepts associated with the label switching control component.

The control component of label switching is responsible for (a) distributing routing information among LSRs and (b) the procedures (algorithms) that these routers use to convert this information into a forwarding table that is used by the label switching forwarding component. Just like a control component of any routing system, the label switching control component must provide for consistent distribution of routing information among LSRs as well as consistent procedures for constructing forwarding tables out of this information.

There is a great deal of similarity between the control component of the conventional routing architecture and the label switching control component. In fact, the label switching control component includes all the routing protocols (e.g., OSPF, BGP, PIM, and so forth) used by the control component of the conventional routing architecture. In this sense the control component of the conventional routing architecture forms a part (subset) of the label switching control component.

However, the control component of the conventional routing architecture is not sufficient to support label switching. This is because the information provided by the control component of the conventional routing architecture isn't sufficient to construct forwarding tables used by the label switching forwarding component, as these tables have to contain mappings between labels and next hops.

To fill the void we need procedures by which an LSR can

a. Create bindings between labels and FECs

b. Inform other LSRs of the bindings it creates

c. Utilize both (a) and (b) to construct and maintain the forwarding table used by the label switching component

The overall structure of the label switching control component is shown in Figure 2.6.

The network layer routing protocols provide LSRs with the mapping between FECs and next hop addresses. Procedures for creating label binding between labels and FECs, and for distributing this binding information among label switches, provide LSRs with the mapping between FECs and labels. The two mappings combined provide the information needed to construct the forwarding tables used by the label switching forwarding component (see Figure 2.7).

Network layer routing protocols (e.g., OSPF, BGP, PIM)	Procedures for creating binding between labels and FECs	Procedures for distributing information about created label bindings
Maintenance of forwarding table		

Figure 2.6 *The label switching control component.*

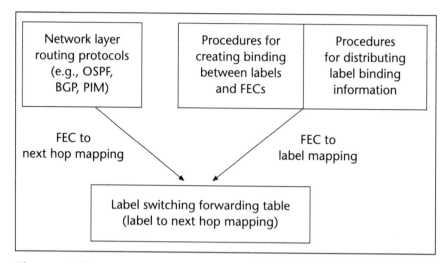

Figure 2.7   *Construction of a label switching forwarding table.*

2.3.1 *Local Versus Remote Binding*

Recall that each entry in a forwarding table maintained by an LSR contains one incoming label and one or more outgoing labels. Corresponding to these two types of labels in the forwarding table, the label switching control component provides two types of label bindings. The first type of label binding occurs when the router creates the binding with a label that is chosen and assigned locally. We refer to such binding as local. The second type of label binding is when the router receives from some other LSR label binding information that corresponds to the label binding created by that other router. We refer to such binding as remote.

An important difference between a local and a remote binding is that with the local binding the label associated with the binding is chosen locally, by the LSR itself, whereas with the remote binding the label associated with the binding is chosen by some other LSR.

2.3.2 *Upstream Versus Downstream Binding*

The label switching control component uses both local and remote bindings to populate its forwarding table with incoming and outgoing labels. This could be done in two ways. The first method is when labels from the local binding are used as incoming labels, and labels from the remote binding are used as outgoing labels. The second is exactly the opposite—labels from the local binding are used as outgoing labels, and labels from the remote binding are used as incoming labels. We examine each option in turn.

The first option is called *downstream* label binding because binding between a label carried by a packet and a particular FEC that the packet belongs to is created by an LSR that is downstream (with respect to the flow of the packet) from the LSR that places the label in the packet. Observe that with downstream label binding, packets that carry a particular label flow in the direction opposite to the flow of the binding information about that label.

The second option is called *upstream* label binding because binding between a label carried by a packet and a particular FEC that the packet belongs to is created by the same LSR that places the label in the packet; that is, the creator of the binding is upstream with respect to the flow of packets. Observe that with upstream label binding, packets that carry a particular label flow in the same direction as the label binding information about this label.

The names *upstream* and *downstream* seem to have caused considerable confusion, but no attempt to come up with less confusing names has yet succeeded. We have found that it helps to consider the flow of data packets—they flow toward the downstream end of the link—and then ask the question "At which end of the link were the bindings created: upstream or downstream?" Figure 2.8 illustrates flow of both data packets and label binding information for the downstream and upstream label binding modes. In each case data packets flow "down" to the right. In downstream allocation, binding is generated at the downstream end of the link; with upstream allocation, binding is generated at the upstream end.

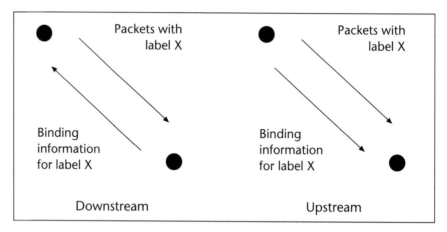

Figure 2.8 *Downstream versus upstream label binding.*

2.3.3 *"Free" Labels*

An LSR maintains a pool of "free" labels (labels with no bindings). When the LSR is first initialized, the pool contains all possible labels that the LSR can use for local binding. The size of this pool ultimately determines how many concurrent label bindings the LSR will be able to support. When the router creates a new local binding, the router takes a label from the pool; when the router destroys a previously created binding, the router returns the label associated with that binding to the pool.

Recall that an LSR could maintain either a single forwarding table or multiple forwarding tables—one per interface. When the router maintains a single label switching forwarding table, the router maintains a single pool of labels. When the LSR maintains a label switching table on a per-interface basis, the LSR maintains pools of labels on a per-interface basis as well.

2.3.4 *Creating and Destroying Label Binding: Control-Driven Versus Data-Driven Label Binding*

An LSR creates or destroys a binding between a label and an FEC as a result of a particular event. Such an event could be triggered by either data packets that have to be forwarded by the LSR, or by control (routing) information (e.g., OSPF routing updates, PIM JOIN/PRUNE messages, RSVP PATH/RESV messages) that has to be processed by the LSR. When the creation or destruction of bindings is triggered by data packets, we refer to it as *data-driven* label binding. When the creation or destruction of bindings is triggered by control information, we refer to it as *control-driven* label binding.

There is a wide range of options within both data-driven and control-driven approaches. For example, a data-driven approach might create a binding to an application's flow as soon as it sees the first packet for a flow, or it might wait until it has seen several packets, suggesting that the flow is long enough to warrant creation of a binding.

One attractive property of data-driven label binding is that it creates a binding only when there is data traffic that could utilize this binding—label binding is created on demand. As a result, with data-driven label binding one could expect that all other factors being equal, the total number of entries in the label switching forwarding table of an LSR would be less than with control-driven binding. It is certainly true that all other factors being equal, the total number of entries in the forwarding table with the data-driven binding would be no more than with the control-driven label binding. Whether it will be less, and how much less, would depend very much on the data traffic pattern. Because the data traffic pattern depends on a variety of factors (e.g., the set of applications), and because some of these factors exhibit a high degree of variability, it is not clear whether one could build a system that is robust enough with respect to changes in the traffic pattern, while at the same time able to exploit this potential advantage of data-driven label binding.

Data-driven label binding also has some drawbacks compared to control-driven label binding. First of all, the amount of control traffic needed to distribute label binding information may be higher than that needed with control-driven label binding. This is because with data-driven label binding, the binding information needs to be distributed in response to both changes in the FEC to next hop mapping, as well as in response to changes in data traffic (as label binding is created and destroyed as a consequence of changes in data traffic). In contrast, with control-driven label binding, binding information is distributed only in response to changes in the FEC to next hop mapping.

Second, data-driven label binding assumes that an LSR supports both the label switching forwarding component, as well as the conventional routing forwarding component. Supporting the conventional routing forwarding component is needed because label binding is created as a side effect of conventional forwarding of a packet. In contrast, with control-driven label binding an LSR may not be required to support the conventional routing forwarding component at all, as creation and destruction of label binding doesn't involve conventional forwarding of packets.

With data-driven label binding, if forwarding performance of the conventional routing forwarding component is less than the performance of the label switching forwarding component, then the overall forwarding performance may be inferior compared to that with control-driven label binding. This is because, with the control-driven label binding, label bindings are precomputed, and thus all the packets could be forwarded by the label switching forwarding component.

Use of data-driven label binding also complicates the overall system behavior, because the operations of the control component are controlled by a mix of control and data traffic, whereas with control-driven label binding the operations of the control component are controlled solely by the control traffic.

2.3.5 *Distributing Label Binding Information: What Are the Options?*

Once an LSR creates or destroys a binding between a locally chosen label and an FEC, the LSR needs to inform other LSRs of that
binding; this will provide other LSRs with the remote label binding information. Distributing label binding information can be
accomplished in several ways.

Piggyback on Top of Routing Protocols

One way to distribute label binding information is to piggyback
this information on top of the routing protocols. This approach is
only possible in control-driven schemes, because it ties label distribution to the distribution of control (routing) information, and
has some attractive properties. First of all, it makes distribution of
label binding information consistent with the distribution of the
routing information. It also allows race conditions to be avoided,
where either the label binding information (binding between
labels and FECs) would be available, but the associated routing
information (and, more specifically, the binding between FECs
and next hops) would not, or vice versa. Finally, it simplifies the
overall system operation, as it eliminates the need for a separate
protocol to distribute label binding information.

However, this approach has drawbacks as well. First of all, the
routing information that is distributed by a particular protocol
may not be suitable for distributing label binding information—
only the protocols where distributed routing information explicitly contains mapping between FECs and next hops would be suitable for piggybacking label binding information. For this reason
Link-State Routing protocols (e.g., OSPF) make a rather poor
match for what is required to distribute label binding information.
On the other hand, for precisely the same reason, protocols such
as BGP and PIM seem to be quite suitable for distributing label
binding information as well.

Even if the routing information distributed by a protocol makes
the protocol suitable for the distribution of label binding information, extending the protocol to carry this information may not
always be feasible. This is because extending the protocol may

involve changes to the format of the messages used by the protocol, which, in turn, may result in backward incompatibility. So,
even if one views the option of piggybacking the label binding
information on top of the routing protocol as desirable, it may not
always be feasible.

Label Distribution Protocol

Constraining label switching to only the cases where the routing
protocols can piggyback label binding information is undesirable.
A way to circumvent this limitation is by distributing label binding information via a separate protocol.

The ability to support label switching with routing protocols
that can't be used for piggybacking label binding information is
perhaps the major advantage of using a separate label distribution
protocol. But it is likely to be the only advantage of this approach.

On the negative side this approach makes it more difficult to
avoid race conditions—one may end up in a situation where an
LSR would have label binding information (label to FEC binding),
but not the routing information (FEC to next hop binding)
needed to use the label binding information, or vice versa.

Another drawback of this approach is that it introduces yet
another protocol into the system, which increases the overall
complexity of the system.

If the label switching control component uses only one label
distribution protocol, then this approach also makes it hard to
make distribution of label binding information consistent with
the distribution of routing information. To see why this is true,
observe that while some of the routing protocols exchange routing information based on the technique of incremental updates
and explicit acknowledgments (e.g., BGP), other routing protocols
use periodic refreshes of complete routing information (e.g., PIM).

A way to avoid this mismatch is to have more than one label
distribution protocol. With this method you could make one label
distribution protocol that will be used in conjunction with OSPF
and will rely on incremental updates and explicit acknowledgments, while making another label distribution protocol that will
be used in conjunction with PIM and will rely on periodic

refreshes of complete binding information. But though this approach would solve the problem of consistent distribution of label binding information, it would introduce even more protocols into the system, which in turn would result in an even more complex system.

Based on the above discussion, the option of piggybacking label binding information on top of routing protocols should be viewed as preferred whenever possible or feasible; a separate label distribution protocol should be used only when piggybacking is not possible or feasible. By limiting the scope where a label distribution protocol is needed, one could hope to either reduce or avoid mismatch between the distribution of label binding information and the distribution of routing information while at the same time being able to stay with a single label distribution protocol.

2.3.6 *Independent Versus Ordered Creation of Forwarding Entries*

An entry in a label switching forwarding table is created by a combination of the following:

- Next hop: This is provided by routing protocols as an FEC to next hop mapping.

- Incoming label: With downstream binding this is provided by creating a local binding between an FEC and the label; with upstream binding this is provided by receiving a remote binding between an FEC and the label.

- Outgoing label: With downstream binding this is provided by a remote binding between an FEC and the label; with upstream binding this is provided by creating a local binding between an FEC and the label.

Because different pieces of the information needed to construct an entry are supplied by different parts of the label switching control component, one important issue is the amount of coordination that should be imposed on these parts.

In Section 2.3.5 we encountered a situation where not all pieces of the information needed to construct an entry would be available to an LSR at the same time. If the distribution of label binding information is accomplished via a separate label distribution protocol (rather than piggybacking this information on top of a routing protocol), the information about FEC to next hop mapping (provided by the routing protocol) could arrive either before or after the arrival of the remote label binding information. Piggybacking label binding information on top of routing protocols provides a very simple and inexpensive (in terms of the overhead) mechanism to coordinate the arrival of routing with the arrival of remote label binding information. However, as we discussed before, piggybacking may not always be a feasible option.

When the remote label binding information is distributed via a separate label distribution protocol, an LSR could create the local label binding either as soon as the FEC to next hop mapping becomes available to the LSR, or only when both the FEC to next hop mapping and the remote binding information become available. We refer to the former option as *independent*, and to the latter as *ordered* creation of forwarding table entries.

The most important distinction between the independent and ordered creation of forwarding table entries is this: with independent creation, once an LSR receives the FEC to next hop mapping and creates (in response to that mapping) the local label binding, the LSR may advertise this binding to other LSRs, thus providing other LSRs with the remote label binding. In contrast, with ordered creation, even if an LSR receives the FEC to next hop mapping and creates its local label binding, the LSR has to wait until it receives the appropriate remote label binding before it can start advertising its local label binding to other LSRs.

Use of ordered versus independent creation of forwarding table entries has certain implications on the overall system behavior. First of all, the ordered creation adds latency to the construction of forwarding entries by LSRs, because it serializes the creation of such entries among a set of LSRs. With the independent creation an LSR may establish its forwarding entries in parallel with other LSRs. Second, the ordered creation creates additional interdependencies among LSRs, which in turn brings robustness and scalability problems. In contrast, the independent creation minimizes such interdependencies. On the other hand, if one wants to have label switching for some, but not all, FECs (so that packets that map only into certain FECs would be label switched), and one is able to control this via configuration management, the ordered creation simplifies network management by reducing the number of devices that have to be configured with the information about which FECs should be label switched.

2.3.7 *Multicast Considerations*

Supporting multicast forwarding with label switching places certain requirements on the label switching control component. In this section we look at some of these requirements.

Multicast routing uses spanning trees[1] for forwarding of multicast packets, where a tree could be associated with either a combination of a particular source and multicast group (source-based tree), or just with a particular group (shared tree). We refer to such trees as *multicast distribution trees*.

To provide consistent forwarding of multicast packets with label switching, an LSR, when it receives a packet, must be able to unambiguously identify a particular multicast distribution tree that the LSR should use to forward the packet. To identify a particular multicast distribution tree, the only information provided by a packet to an LSR is (a) a label carried in a packet and (b) an interface that the packet arrived on. Relying on just a combination of a label and an incoming interface for identifying a particular tree requires that an LSR maintains its label switching table on a per-interface basis.

---

[1] The spanning trees we refer to in this section should not be confused with spanning trees constructed by bridges. The former are constructed by network layer multicast procedures (e.g., PIM); the latter are constructed by link layer procedures (e.g., IEEE 802.1).

When a multiaccess link layer technology has native multicast capabilities (e.g., Ethernet), label switching must be able to utilize these capabilities. Such utilization requires that a group of LSRs that are all connected to a common multiaccess subnetwork with native multicast capabilities and are part of a common multicast distribution tree agree on a common label to use for that particular tree. To support this the label switching control component must include (a) procedures for electing one particular LSR within the group that will be responsible for creating label binding and (b) procedures for distributing this label binding information to the rest of the LSRs in the group.

When an LSR connected to a multiaccess subnetwork (e.g., Ethernet) receives a multicast packet, the LSR has to identify a particular multicast distribution tree that should be used to determine how to handle the packet. To identify the tree, the LSR has to identify the previous hop LSR that sent the packet. This, in turn, requires that no two LSRs connected to a common multiaccess subnetwork can use a combination of the same label and the same interface for creating label bindings for different multicast distribution trees. One way to accomplish this is to partition the set of labels that can be used for multicast by a set of LSRs connected to a common multiaccess subnetwork into disjoint subsets and to give each LSR its own subset. The LSR would use such a subset as its pool of free labels that is associated with the interface that connects the router to the subnetwork. We will see an example of this approach in Chapter 5.

2.3.8 *Handling Routing Transients*

We use the term *routing transient* to refer to episodes in a network where routing information across a network is changing. At such times, information stored at different nodes may be temporarily inconsistent. These episodes most commonly occur as a result of failures of links or routers or both.

Although all of the routing protocols used by conventional routing guarantee loop-free paths in a steady state, almost all of them (with the exception of EIGRP[2]) can't guarantee loop-free paths during routing transients. Clearly, using these protocols as part of the label switching control component does nothing to alter this situation. Therefore, label switching, just like conventional routing, needs to have mechanism(s) to deal with the adverse effects of forwarding loops during routing transients.

The major adverse effect caused by a forwarding loop is excessive consumption of networking resources (e.g., buffers on routers, CPU on routers, bandwidth) by packets that are forwarded along the loop. This, in turn, may result in the lack of resources needed to handle other packets. Especially detrimental to the overall system could be the lack of resources needed to handle packets that carry routing information (control traffic). At the minimum this would slow down the convergence of the routing system, thus prolonging the duration of routing transients and therefore forwarding loops caused by these transients. Even worse, the lack of resources needed to handle packets that carry routing information may cause routing instabilities. Also detrimental to the overall system, although to a lesser degree, is the lack of resources needed to handle noncontrol traffic for which nonlooping paths are available.

One way to deal with the adverse effects of forwarding loops during routing transients is to make sure that when a forwarding loop is formed, no traffic enters such a loop. In this book we refer to this as *loop prevention*. Another alternative is to allow traffic to enter the loop but to constrain the amount of resources that can be consumed by such traffic. In this book we refer to this as *loop mitigation*.

All other factors being equal, loop prevention may be viewed as more desirable than loop mitigation. However, all other factors aren't equal. When comparing loop prevention and loop mitigation mechanisms, we need to look at such issues as (a) the overhead in terms of additional control traffic, (b) scalability, (c)

---

[2] EIGRP (enhanced interior gateway routing protocol) is a Cisco proprietary intradomain routing protocol that employs the "DUAL" algorithm for loop avoidance.

negative impact (if any) introduced by such mechanisms on the nonlooping traffic, and (d) the ability to contain the negative impact of the looping traffic on the nonlooping traffic (and especially on the control traffic).

Conventional routing employs loop mitigation as the way to deal with the adverse effects of forwarding loops during routing transients. Loop mitigation is achieved via the time-to-live mechanism, where the network layer header contains a field, called time-to-live (TTL). A router that forwards a packet decrements this field by 1. If a router receives a packet whose time-to-live value is 0, the router discards the packet. This way, even if a packet enters a forwarding loop, the number of times the packet would be able to circle the loop is bounded—eventually the time-to-live field in the packet will reach 0, and the packet will be discarded.

Because the forwarding path taken by a packet may include both LSRs, as well as conventional routers, it is important that the mechanisms used by the LSRs to deal with forwarding loops during routing transients be able to coexist and interoperate with the mechanisms used by the conventional routers. In practical terms that means that the mechanisms used by the LSRs must be able to coexist and interoperate with the time-to-live mechanism.

A way to make the mechanisms used by the LSRs to deal with forwarding loops during routing transients coexist and interoperate with the time-to-live mechanism is to have the LSRs use the time-to-live mechanism as well. Unfortunately this may be fairly difficult to achieve when label switching is used over certain link layer technologies, most notably ATM and Frame Relay. This is because neither the ATM nor the Frame Relay header contains the TTL field, and neither ATM nor Frame Relay switches are capable of handling the TTL field carried in the network layer header. On the other hand, if a label isn't carried in the link layer header, but in a shim label header, one could add the TTL field to the shim header, thus making it possible for label switching to use the time-to-live mechanism to deal with forwarding loops during routing transients.

The alternative to using TTL for loop mitigation is to use additional control mechanisms in LSRs either to prevent or to mitigate loops. We will see examples of all these approaches in the following chapters.

2.4 Edge Devices

So far we have described how LSRs forward packets that carry labels. But how do these packets get their labels in the first place? Turning "unlabeled" packets into "labeled" ones and vice versa is performed by the edge LSRs.

One can think of an edge LSR as a device that implements the control and forwarding components of both the label switching and conventional routing. When an edge LSR receives a packet without a label, the LSR uses the conventional forwarding component to determine the FEC that this packet belongs to and the next hop that the packet should be sent to. If the next hop is an LSR, then the LSR uses the label switching forwarding component to determine the label that should be added to the packet. Likewise, when an edge LSR receives a packet with a label, the LSR uses the label switching forwarding component to determine the FEC that this packet belongs to and the next hop that the packet should be sent to. If the next hop is not an LSR, then the LSR just strips the label from the packet and hands the packet to its conventional forwarding component, which, in turn, sends the packet to the next hop.

The fact that both LSRs and conventional routers use the same set of routing protocols makes interworking between the conventional and the label switching control components trivial. The only thing that is required of the label switching control component is the ability to determine whether a particular (next hop) router is an LSR or not.

In some cases, a host may function as the edge device. Because hosts do not generally run routing protocols, there are some additional challenges to making a host capable of applying labels to packets. We return to this subject in Chapter 4.

2.5 Relationship Between Label Switching and Network Layer Addressing and Routing

Label switching replaces forwarding algorithms used by various routing functions with a single forwarding component. At the same time label switching doesn't replace procedures for establishing and maintaining routing information—label switching assumes the use of the existing procedures, such as OSPF, BGP, and so forth. Likewise, label switching doesn't replace the need for network layer (e.g., IP) addressing, as the network layer addressing information forms an essential part of routing information, and this information is used by the label switching control component.

2.6 Summary

All approaches to label switching, as we have defined it in this book, have certain common characteristics, and all must make some common design choices. This chapter has introduced the common ground on which the rest of the book builds.

The LSRs used in all the approaches to label switching described in this book implement a control component and a forwarding component. The forwarding component is based on a simple label swapping algorithm and uses fixed-length labels. These labels are used as an index to the label switching table, which identifies where a packet should be forwarded and perhaps some local resource assignment as well. In contrast to conventional routing, the LSRs use the same algorithm no matter what control components are in use.

The control components consist of conventional network layer routing protocols and one or more label binding mechanisms. It is in the area of creating and distributing label bindings that the various approaches show the most diversity. Label bindings may be created by upstream or downstream LSRs; they may be created either in ordered or in independent fashion; they may be created in response to data or control traffic; and the bindings may be distributed in a stand-alone protocol or piggybacked on an existing one.

A few of the trade-offs inherent in the design choices have been briefly introduced here, but more detailed analysis of the trade-offs will be possible once we have examined some of the label switching approaches in detail. The next four chapters provide such an examination.

Further Reading

For an overview of various routing protocols used in the Internet (OSPF, RIP, BGP, PIM, etc.) we recommend

Halabi, B. *Internet Routing Architectures*. Indianapolis: Cisco Press, 1997.

Huitema, C. *Routing in the Internet*. Englewood Cliffs, NJ: Prentice-Hall, 1995.

The protocols OSPF, PIM, BGP, and RSVP are all specified in Internet RFCs:

Braden, R., L. Zhang, S. Berson, S. Herzog, and S. Jamin. *Resource ReSerVation Protocol (RSVP): Version 1 Functional Specification*. RFC 2209, September 1997.

Estrin, D., et al. *Protocol Independent Multicast-Sparse Mode (PIM-SM): Protocol Specification*. RFC 2117, June 1997.

Moy, J. *OSPF Version 2*. RFC 1583, March 1994.

Rekhter, Y., and T. Li. *A Border Gateway Protocol 4 (BGP-4)*. RFC 1771, March 1995.

The DUAL algorithm for loop prevention is described in

Garcia-Luna-Aceves, J. J. "A Unified Approach to Loop-free Routing Using Distance Vectors or Link States." *Computer Communications Review* 19, no. 4, September 1989.

Chapter

3

The Cell Switching Router (CSR)

In this chapter and the next three we look at four of the proposed approaches to label switching, proceeding in the order in which they were publicly announced. The first of these is the Cell Switching Router, or CSR, as specified and developed primarily by Toshiba.

As we observed in Chapter 1, one way to build a label switching router is to run IP control protocols directly on ATM switching hardware. The CSR, as the name suggests, is such an approach. All label switching approaches also require a label binding protocol, and the one used by the CSR is the Flow Attribute Notification Protocol (FANP).

CSR predates the Multiprotocol Label Switching (MPLS) initiative by several years. It was presented to the IETF IP over ATM working group in spring 1994 and to the ATM Forum's Service Aspects and Applications working group in the summer of that year. The CSR was presented again at an IETF BOF (Birds of a Feather) session in spring 1995. When the effort to charter the MPLS working group began in late 1996, the CSR was presented as one of the candidate approaches to label switching (along with Tag Switching and ARIS).

The delay between the first presentations of the CSR approach and the formation of a working group to standardize label switching seems surprisingly long. No doubt there were many factors at work, not least of which was that it took some time for a critical mass of companies to become interested in the idea. As we discussed in Chapter 1, the motivations for label switching are many and varied, and it certainly was not apparent at the outset that there were so many reasons to pursue this technology.

Because the CSR was initially proposed as a solution to the IP/ATM integration problem discussed in Section 1.1.3, and because all the other approaches described in this book also aim to address that issue, we begin this chapter with some background material on IP, ATM, and IP over ATM. Readers familiar with these technologies may wish to skip ahead to Section 3.2, where we provide an overview of the CSR approach. Section 3.3 presents details of FANP, the label binding protocol of this approach.

3.1 ATM and IP Essentials

For the purposes of this chapter, and indeed of this book, the important things about ATM that we need to be aware of are that it is a virtual circuit (VC)–based technology that uses fixed-length packets called *cells*. Variable-length packet data is adapted to the fixed-length cell transport using ATM adaptation layers (AALs). Both the adaptation to ATM and the switching of cells from one VC to another commonly take place in hardware. Because the cell switching is done in relatively simple hardware, it has proved possible to build fast and cheap ATM switches.

To understand the motivation behind CSR/FANP, it is helpful to be familiar with the role of subnets and subnet addresses in the IP architecture. Also we need to understand how the classical IP over ATM model preserves this architecture and why this model was viewed by many, including the Toshiba team, to be unsatisfactory.

In this section we explain these aspects of ATM and IP to lay the groundwork for the following discussion of CSR and FANP. Readers familiar with the concepts mentioned in the previous two paragraphs may wish to skip ahead to Section 3.1.3, in which we explain the classical IP over ATM model and the restrictions it imposes. Those who understand these restrictions may proceed directly to Section 3.2.

3.1.1 *Cells, ATM Adaptation Layers, and Virtual Circuits*

IP datagrams are an example of variable-length packet data. Applications generating IP packets may, within certain limits, make them any size they want and may vary that size at (almost) any time. A field in the header of each IP packet indicates the length of that particular packet. In contrast, ATM uses fixed-length packets called *cells*. ATM cells consist of a 5-octet header and a 48-octet information field. The exact form of the ATM cell header depends on the interface[1] it is passing across.

If we wish to carry IP datagrams over an ATM network, we need a means to get the variable-length packets into and out of the fixed-length cells. This is exactly the role of the ATM adaptation layer (AAL). Different AALs exist for the different types of traffic that need to be mapped to ATM. For variable-length packet data AAL number five (AAL5) is most commonly used. AAL5 allows variable-length packets to be segmented into cells and subsequently reassembled back into packets. The segmentation and reassembly (SAR) operations of AAL5 are almost always performed in dedicated hardware called SAR devices. Figure 3.1 illustrates segmentation. The original datagram is segmented into 48-byte segments, each of which is then placed in the information field of a cell and the header is attached. Note that this leads to a "train" of cells whose total length is longer than that of the original datagram (because of the ATM cell headers). Reassembly should be easy to visualize looking at this diagram also; the cell headers are removed and the segments are concatenated in order to reconstruct the original datagram.

---

[1] Interfaces are defined between users (e.g., hosts) and the network, the user to network interface (UNI), and between network elements (e.g., switches), the network to network interface (NNI).

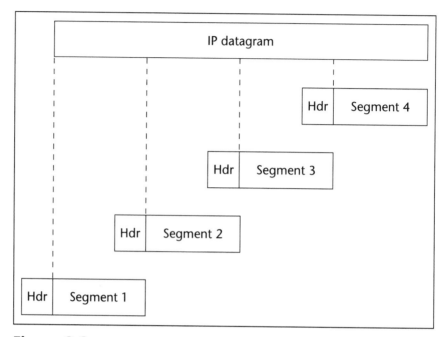

Figure 3.1 *Segmenting a datagram. Each segment is placed in the information field of a cell.*

Another important characteristic of ATM is that it is a virtual circuit (VC) technology. One physical link can be logically considered as many separate virtual links (or circuits), with each cell that travels on a physical link belonging to one VC. Two of the fields in the 5-byte ATM cell header, the virtual path identifier (VPI) and virtual circuit identifier (VCI), together indicate to which VC a particular cell belongs. (The fact that there are two fields rather than one is a detail that need not concern us right now.) Figure 3.2 shows a simplified version of the ATM cell at the user to network interface (UNI) and illustrates three cells, belonging to two different virtual circuits. The fact that the VPI and VCI fields in the header are of fixed length and position, combined with the fixed size of the cells, makes it simple and efficient and therefore, we hope, cheap to build hardware to switch these cells.

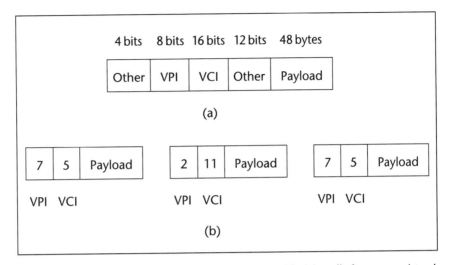

Figure 3.2 *An ATM cell with VCI and VPI fields (a); cells from two virtual circuits (b).*

A network that uses virtual circuits is often referred to as being *connection oriented*. This contrasts with IP, which is based on a connectionless model. We have seen how a single ATM link between two systems can carry cells from different connections, with each one identified by a VCI/VPI. End to end connections across ATM networks are obtained by transferring cells from one of these VCs on one link to another VC on another link using an ATM switch. The resulting connection between the two end systems, which may span many different links and switches, is called a virtual circuit connection (VCC). It is important to realize that while the VCI/VPI information can be used by the systems at either end of a single link to determine which VCC the cell belongs to, the VCI/VPI does not generally remain constant all along the connection. Instead it will usually be rewritten by an ATM switch as it forwards the cell. Thus VCIs and VPIs can be said to have *link local* (rather than global) significance; only the systems at the two ends of a link have to agree what a particular VCI or VPI means.

Within an ATM switch there is a logical data structure, which we call the *switch table*, that maps incoming port and cell VPI/VCI to outgoing port and cell VPI/VCI. Typically this switch table is implemented in some slightly more complex form, perhaps as separate tables for each port, in very fast memory in the switch. As each cell arrives, the hardware looks up or "indexes" this table using the incoming port and then the VPI/VCI in the cell header to find which output port to send the cell to and what VPI/VCI to place in the cell header when the cell is sent out onto the link connected to that port.

Table 3.1 shows an excerpt from a switch table of the sort we have described. Imagine a cell arriving on port 1 with VPI equal to 57 and VCI equal to 68. By looking up these properties of the cell in the table, we find that the third row contains the relevant information. The three rightmost columns state that the cell must be sent out port 2 with the VPI set to 57 and the VCI set to 91. The great speed of commercial ATM switches is achieved by using specialized hardware to perform the lookup and cell header rewrite that we have just done on paper. In the five seconds or so that it took you to look up the table a commercial switch could have performed the operation about 20 million times.

Table 3.1 ATM switch table.

In port	VPI	VCI	Out port	VPI	VCI
1	83	67	5	3	33
1	34	125	5	21	125
1	57	68	2	57	91
2	9	56	6	34	55
2	21	64	1	36	38
5	3	68	5	45	89
5	45	128	2	81	125

At this point we should recognize that the process just described to forward cells in an ATM switch bears a strong resemblance to the label swapping forwarding algorithm described in the preceding chapter. It is because of this that there is so much interest in using ATM switches as label switching routers.

It should be obvious that to set up an end to end VCC there has to be cooperation between the two end points and all the switches along the path between them to ensure that all systems have consistent views of the VCI and VPI that are used on each link in the path. This cooperation can be achieved in one of two ways:

- By management, that is, by an operator installing consistent data in all the systems along the path to set up the desired switch tables. A connection set up this way is referred to as a permanent virtual connection (PVC).

- By signalling, that is, the use of a dynamic mechanism in which messages pass from end to end along the path establishing the required switch state. We refer to connections set up in this manner as switched virtual circuits (SVC).

In either case, the end result is that the switch tables throughout the network are set up correctly to forward cells from end to end along the VCC. Another point to note about the setting up of virtual circuit connections is that, to create a connection, it is necessary to specify the end points of the connection. The end points have addresses, and these addresses (which are much longer than VCIs and have global scope in the network) have to be assigned according to some addressing scheme. ATM uses two addressing schemes, referred to as E.164 and NSAP addressing. It is not important to know much about these addressing schemes except to note that they are both different from IP addressing, which is one of the issues that an IP over ATM network needs to deal with.

3.1.2 *IP Addresses and Subnets*

IP was designed to be able to operate over a wide range of data link layer (layer 2) technologies. The ubiquity of IP in internetworking today is a testament to that design and to the labors of the IETF, which, as new data link layer technologies have emerged, has worked out how to run IP over them. Not surprisingly, with an important technology such as ATM a lot of effort has been expended to do this. In fact work is still ongoing (as of the time of writing) in this area. We briefly described the first widely adopted solution to this problem, the classical IP over ATM approach, in Chapter 1. As we saw there, the classical IP over ATM model described in RFC 1577 relied on the concept of a logical IP subnet (LIS). To better understand this concept, it will help to look a little more closely at IP addressing and routing.

The IP address is a 32-bit number and is interpreted as two parts. One identifies a network and the other a host (end system) within that network. The situation has become a little more complicated than this in recent years, since the concept of *subnetting* was introduced to deal with growth in the number of hosts and networks, but that doesn't affect the issues here significantly. For the purposes of this simple discussion we can continue to think of the address as having two parts, a network part and a host part. Each subnet has a subnet mask that defines how long each part of the address is. For example, if the subnet mask is 255.255.255.0, which in binary is 24 ones followed by 8 zeroes, then the network is identified by the first 24 bits of the address, and the host part by the last 8 bits.

When a host wants to send a packet to another host, it can figure out if that host is on the same subnet by looking at the destination address of that host and seeing if the network part matches the network part of its own address. For example, a host with address 171.69.210.11 and a subnet mask of 255.255.255.0 is on the same subnet as a host with address 171.69.210.30, but is on a different subnet from a host with address 171.69.212.40. The main reason to care if another host is on the same subnet or not is to determine whether it is possible to reach the other host directly: if it's on the same subnet, it is possible; if not, it is necessary to go through a router.

This is a fundamental architectural feature of IP. To reach a host on another network or subnet, traffic is sent via a router. This model maps well to an internetwork where the router also performs the function of transferring datagrams from one link layer technology to another, for example, from an Ethernet to an asynchronous serial line.

3.1.3 *IP over ATM*

RFC 1577 defines how to make IP work on an ATM network. It does not attempt to change the addressing or routing model of IP, but it does allow for the fact that a single ATM network might be broken up into several different logical IP subnets (LISs). Logical IP subnets are defined in much the same way as they were above: hosts and routers that have the same value to the network part of their address are on the same subnet. But why should an ATM network be divided into a number of LISs in the first place? There are several reasons, including security and address allocation. For example, because routers must be used by all packets passing from one subnet to another, routers are used to provide a degree of isolation between networks. It is also difficult to coordinate address allocation over a very large network without somehow partitioning the address space and letting different administrative groups control portions of the space. Subnets are a logical way to handle this.

Note that classical IP over ATM requires all traffic between LISs to pass through a router, even when those LISs are part of the same ATM network and thus could in principle be directly interconnected by a virtual circuit. This condition was viewed by many to be a significant drawback of the model. At the time this model was developed, routers were seriously lagging ATM switches in areas such as throughput, latency, and quality of service capabilities. Even within a single organization, where one might allow any to any connectivity without concern for security, the classical model's requirement for routers significantly affected the performance characteristics of the overall network.

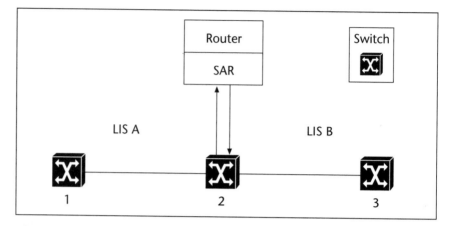

Figure 3.3   *One-armed router connecting two LISs. The router is a member of both LIS A and LIS B.*

The use of a router to interconnect two LISs is illustrated in Figure 3.3. A conventional router, equipped with an ATM interface, connects to the ATM network at one point and is thus referred to as a *one-armed router*. In order for it to forward packets from LIS A to LIS B, it must reassemble the cell stream, perform its forwarding function on the reassembled packets, and then segment the cell stream. This limits the performance of the whole fabric for the inter-LIS communication to that available from the conventional router; in addition, segmentation and reassembly is performed at every such router, adding latency and perhaps further performance overhead.

The CSR/FANP proposal was motivated primarily by the desire to remove the overhead of sending traffic through a conventional router when it passes between LISs. The goal was to allow ATM switches (with, of course, the appropriate IP software) to switch the IP traffic. Unlike the rest of the approaches in this book, it did not seek to do away with the classical model altogether.

3.2 CSR Overview

Like all the label switching approaches described in this book, CSR uses label swapping forwarding combined with IP control protocols and a label distribution mechanism. Like all the other approaches, it can operate on standard ATM switch hardware. Although it could be extended to other types of hardware and links, such extensions have not been publicly specified at the time of writing. Unlike the other approaches, it does not try to do away with standard ATM signalling and RFC 1577. In fact, one of the major motivations for CSR seems to have been the desire to solve the inter-LIS communication problem described above.

To understand how a CSR deals with inter-LIS communication, consider the fact that, from a control point of view, a CSR looks very much like a router. Thus, it can interconnect subnets in the classical model. However, from a forwarding point of view, it behaves just like an ATM switch, since a CSR can be built using standard ATM switch hardware. Thus, it does not introduce any of the performance issues associated with one-armed routers.

The CSR specifications define three types of VC: *default, dedicated,* and *cut-through*. In the initial state, a pair of CSRs communicate over the default VC and all traffic between them—routing protocols, data traffic, and so forth—flows over this VC. A dedicated VC is one that carries an individual flow only, for example, traffic belonging to a single application, which could be identified by a quintuple of the form <source address, destination address, protocol, source port, destination port>. (We will have more to say about the definition of flows later in this chapter and the next.) A cut-through VC is one that is made by splicing together, at a CSR, two dedicated VCs. Although standard ATM VCs are usually bidirectional, it is worth noting that, in the CSR, only the default VC is used in this way. Dedicated and cut-through VCs, because they carry individual flows, are used in one direction only. These three types of VC are illustrated in Figure 3.4.

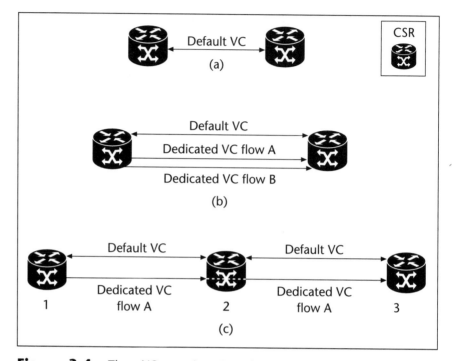

Figure 3.4   *Three VC types in a CSR: default VC (a); dedicated VCs (b); and cut-through VC (c—formed at CSR 2).*

Initially all IP traffic between a pair of adjacent CSRs is sent on the default VC. Traffic arriving at a CSR on the default VC is examined, and "flows" are selected (according to some local criteria) from it with the intention of providing cut-through paths for them. As we will discuss further in the next chapter, the process of flow selection is to some extent a local choice at each switch, and thus need not be specified or standardized. In the case of the CSR implementation, the selection of flows is based in part on examination of TCP and UDP port numbers, which in turn identify the application that is sending traffic.

When a CSR receives packets on the default VC, it has to reassemble them just like a conventional router and forward them to the next hop CSR (as determined by normal IP routing) on the default VC. If, however, the packet belongs to a flow that is selected for cut-through, the CSR selects a VC that connects it to the next hop CSR to become the dedicated VC for that particular flow. It uses FANP to tell the next hop CSR about the association between flows and the VCs on which they will arrive. Once a CSR is receiving a certain flow over a dedicated VC and transmitting the same flow on to its next hop over a dedicated VC, it can then set up the cell switching hardware to forward cells from the flow at the ATM level, thereby creating a cut-through VC (also called a *bypass pipe* in CSR documents).

CSRs were originally conceived as the "default routers" required by RFC 1577 for the interconnection of logical IP subnets. However, the benefits gained by just replacing the routers at LIS boundaries with CSRs can be somewhat modest, as Figure 3.5 illustrates. The host on the left sends traffic on the default VC to CSR A, which must reassemble packets for the flow before forwarding them. Similarly CSR B has only one VC to the host on the right, so it too must reassemble packets before forwarding them. Only the transit CSR between A and B is able to set up a cut-through VC and forward traffic at the ATM level. Depending on the topology of the network, there could be more transit CSRs than we have shown.

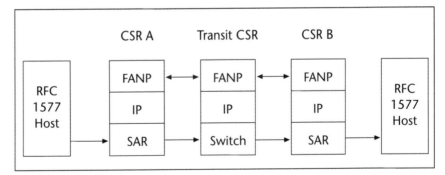

Figure 3.5   *Achieving cut-through in CSRs.*

This is in fact a common feature of all the label switching approaches—there has to be a starting point to the label-switched path, and it is not always possible to push it all the way back to the sending host. Although there are no implementations of FANP running on hosts at the time of writing, it is possible that hosts could participate in FANP to enable a cut-through path to extend all the way to hosts. As we will see in the next chapter, IP Switching does just that with its label binding protocol. Even that approach, however, is only useful for ATM-attached hosts, which are relatively rare.

Another point to note in Figure 3.5 is that there may be standard ATM switches between the CSRs. It is a key feature of the CSR approach that neighboring CSRs may communicate over standard ATM virtual circuits. The next section explains how that is achieved.

3.3 FANP (Flow Attribute Notification Protocol)

We begin this section with some discussion of the operation of the protocol as a whole and conclude with a brief look at each of the protocol messages defined in the specification.

FANP is the label distribution protocol that runs between adjacent CSRs. FANP ensures delivery of protocol messages by using an explicit acknowledgment mechanism with multiple retries built directly into the protocol. FANP messages are, with one exception, transported directly over IP. The single exception—the OFFER protocol message—is sent directly over the link layer. It is claimed that FANP is designed to operate over any connection-oriented data link layer, but the specification and current implementation are restricted to ATM and so we consider only that case here.

Because a primary piece of the motivation for CSRs was to interconnect LISs, the design assumes that CSRs can be overlaid on top of a standard ATM network using RFC 1577. This gives FANP a unique property: it assumes that the native ATM layer labels, the VPI and VCI, cannot be used directly as labels by two neighboring

CSRs. This is because a pair of CSRs, though they may be adjacent in the IP routing sense, may be interconnected by standard ATM VCs. Thus, they can be separated by some number of conventional ATM switches, which of course can rewrite the VPI and VCI fields in the cells.

This problem is solved by having FANP operate in two phases. The first phase is called VCID negotiation. In this phase, a PROPOSE message containing a VCID is sent down a certain VC. The message says, in effect "associate this VCID with the VC on which it arrived." We can think of this as attaching a "handle" to the VC, so that now the CSRs at either end can refer to the VC by its handle. This method works on dynamically signalled switched virtual circuits (SVCs) and on permanent virtual circuits (PVCs) set up by management. Note that the term *negotiation* is slightly misleading, as the process is more like an announcement than a negotiation. This phase is unique among label switching approaches.

In the second phase, the handle is used in OFFER messages to indicate the particular flow that will be sent over the VC. The OFFER messages contain bindings of the form <VCID, FLOWID>. The VCID is the handle just described. The FLOWID is a data element that identifies an IP flow. Currently there is only one flow type defined, of the form <IP source address, IP destination address >. This means that, when a cut-through VC is created, it will carry all traffic between a given pair of hosts.

Recall that the process of deciding to establish a dedicated VC for a certain flow is based on examination of TCP and UDP port numbers. For example, if the well-known TCP port for FTP (the file transfer protocol) is seen, then the CSR may decide to set up a dedicated VC for that flow. However, it can only set up a VC for the pair of hosts involved in the FTP session, and all traffic between those hosts will use that VC. This has some advantages (it reduces the use of VCs) and some disadvantages (in trying to assign quality of service, for example). In any case, it is a feature that could be modified relatively easily by the definition of new FLOWID types.

In looking closely at this two-phase approach, we note that it shows aspects of both hard and soft state. The VCID negotiation phase associates a VCID with a VC. That resulting state is then installed permanently; that is, the protocol does not refresh the VCID information. Thus, the state is *hard*—it will remain forever unless explicitly removed. The reason for this is fairly obvious: once a handle is assigned to a VC, there is no reason to change it as long as the VC remains in place. However, the flows that are sent down a VC may change frequently. Thus the OFFER messages, which bind flows to VCs, use *soft state*—they are resent periodically. CSRs rely on refresh of these messages to "remind" them of the association between flow and VC. If a flow becomes inactive, no refresh is sent, and the association of flow to VC is automatically removed. This is a natural choice, since it is hard to tell when a flow has stopped—the only clue is often the absence of any data for some time period.

The two-phase nature of FANP also illustrates the use of both *inband* and *out of band* signalling. The PROPOSE message is sent on the VC to which it refers, and thus is inband. This is a logical choice, because it provides an easy way to figure out which VC is being identified—the one on which the message was received. All other protocol messages, however, are sent on the default VC, that is, not on the one to which they refer, since by the time they are sent, the VC is clearly identified. Thus they are out of band—sent separately from the data—leaving the dedicated and cut-through VCs free to carry data rather than control messages.

One area in which the CSR documents are somewhat underspecified is in determining how a CSR actually establishes VCs on which to send or receive PROPOSE messages. The FANP documents indicate only that this can be done by "management or signalling." However, this seems like an area where some implementation flexibility is reasonable.

In terms of the taxonomy introduced in Chapter 2, FANP uses an upstream, data-driven and independent model of label allocation. The decision to allocate a label is made locally in response to data traffic and is passed to the downstream neighbor. Label bindings use a separate protocol rather than piggybacking on an existing one.

Another feature to consider in the CSR scheme is IP TTL (time-to-live) handling. In conventional routers, IP TTL is decremented at each hop (and the header checksum adjusted appropriately).

CSRs forwarding IP datagrams as cell streams on a cut-through VC are clearly not capable of performing these functions, because the IP header is not examined when packets flow over a cut-through VC. In contrast to the other proposals we will examine, which take steps to deal with this problem, FANP doesn't address it. Looking again at Figure 3.5, CSRs A and B can process TTL because they are performing full layer 3 routing anyway. When a cut-through VC is established at the transit CSR, however, the TTL is not processed. How big a problem this is, is a subject for debate. We merely observe that a network of CSRs will handle TTL differently from the way that it is handled by "normal" routers. A consequence of this is that, for example, the traceroute tool might not show up all the CSRs on a particular path, and looping packets will take longer to be disposed of.

Having looked at the general properties of the protocol, we now take a look at the message elements of the protocol themselves. First we need to look at the format of the two pieces of information central to the protocol: VCID and FLOWID. We conclude with an examination of the main message types.

3.3.1 *VCID*

We observed above that VCID is used to ensure that two directly connected CSRs can unambiguously identify a VC between them by using the VCID as a handle for the VC. In fact, the VCID is actually more powerful than this: a VCID is a unique number within a single network. A unique value is constructed by appending a locally unique 6-octet value (generated by the system creating the VCID) to its own end system identifier (ESI). The ESI itself is guaranteed to be unique within the network by administrative allocation. The combination of ESI and a locally unique ID is clearly a unique value within the network. Figure 3.6 shows the format of a VCID as it is carried in FANP messages. For this figure and many subsequent ones that show message or packet formats, we adopt the convention of displaying the message as a number of 32-bit (4-byte) words. Thus, in this case, we see the 6-byte ESI occupying the first one and a half words, while the 6-byte ID occupies the second half of the second word and the whole third word. Thus, the whole VCID object is 12 bytes long.

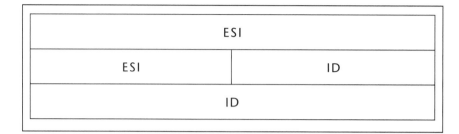

Figure 3.6   *VCID format.*

3.3.2 *FLOWID*

Although the CSR architecture allows for many types of FLOWID, only one is currently defined. It is illustrated in Figure 3.7 and consists of the source and destination IP addresses for the flow (each of which is 32 bits long). As noted above, this doesn't provide the port level granularity that might be expected to enable a dedicated VC to be created for a particular application. On the other hand, the lack of more coarse flow types might be considered a scaling problem, since the number of flows between host pairs in the core of a large network such as the Internet is already large and getting larger.

With pictures of VCID and FLOWID clear in our mind, we can look in turn at the various messages that make up the protocol. The task of a label binding protocol is fairly straightforward, and thus the protocols themselves are relatively simple. FANP provides only three basic operations:

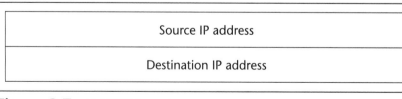

Figure 3.7   *FLOWID format.*

- Associate a VCID with a VC (PROPOSE/PROPOSE ACK)
- Associate a FLOWID with a VCID (OFFER/READY)
- Remove the association between a FLOWID and a VCID (REMOVE/REMOVE ACK)

We briefly describe each of these categories. We have refrained from including detailed message formats here; they can be found in the FANP specification, to which we provide a reference in the "Further Reading" section at the end of this chapter.

3.3.3 PROPOSE/PROPOSE ACK

The purpose of PROPOSE is to allow CSRs to unambiguously identify VCs. This capability is unique to FANP. By employing VCID and the PROPOSE message, CSRs can be interconnected using standard ATM VCs; CSRs do not have to be immediate neighbors of each other at the datalink level.

The PROPOSE message is sent inband on a VC, and it carries the VCID that will subsequently be used to refer to the VC. The PROPOSE ACK that signifies that the other system has received and agrees to use the VCID for the VC is sent back over the "default" VC. Figure 3.8 depicts this sequence.

PROPOSE, as we noted, uses a modified ATMARP format, a somewhat strange choice. The reason, explained to us by the developers, is that they already had the code to deal with this ARP message. Thus a small modification to an existing message format slightly simplified the protocol implementation task.

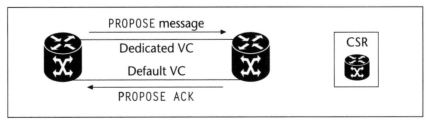

Figure 3.8 PROPOSE/PROPOSE ACK *sequence.*

The "modified" ATMARP message (see RFC 1577 for the original) contains the VCID. Note that this message is sent in a single ATM cell. There is no further encapsulation than to place the message in the payload of an ATM cell. In contrast, PROPOSE ACK is sent on the default VC in an IP datagram. The CSR receiving PROPOSE makes an association between the VC that it arrived on and the VCID value that the PROPOSE contained. This is an example of a piece of hard state. It is remembered for the life of the session between the two CSRs.

3.3.4 *OFFER/READY*

The OFFER message and the READY message sent in acknowledgment to it associate a FLOWID with a VCID. This is the real label binding part of FANP. The CSR that receives an OFFER is able to use the information to map FLOWID via the VCID to the VC (i.e., the VPI/VCI) that traffic for a particular flow (identified by the FLOWID) will arrive on.

Both messages are sent in IP datagrams on the default VC. Both messages carry a VCID and a FLOWID. The OFFER indicates "I'm going to send you traffic for flow x on the VC with VCID y." READY is an acknowledgment that the OFFER message was received and agreed to.

The OFFER message contains a value for a "refresh interval." The downstream CSR retransmits READY at least once per refresh interval while it is still receiving traffic on the VC. This is a simple means of indicating to the upstream CSR that the downstream end is still alive. If no READY is received within a predetermined interval (default six minutes but configurable), then the upstream CSR removes the association between the VCID (and thereby the VC) and the FLOWID. It cannot then transmit on the VC without reissuing an OFFER for the VCID with the same or a different FLOWID. This is a classic example of a time-out mechanism or soft state. Note that the association between VCID and FLOWID can also be removed explicitly, using the REMOVE message described below.

3.3.5 *REMOVE/REMOVE ACK*

The REMOVE message is used to explicitly remove the association between a VCID and a FLOWID. A CSR receiving this message will remove the state in its data structures that map FLOWID via VCID to VC. The mapping between VCID and VC, however, remains unchanged. REMOVE ACK is sent as an acknowledgment that the instruction has been complied with. Both these messages are encapsulated in IP datagrams.

3.3.6 *ERROR*

Finally we come to one of the most useful messages in any protocol. Announcer of broken machines and broken implementations but not, we hope, of broken protocol design: the ERROR message. Precisely what bad thing has happened is indicated in the ERROR code field.

3.4 Summary

The CSR/FANP approach was the first label switching technique to be publicly specified. Although it is claimed to be generally applicable to connection-oriented datalinks it is clear that at this time it applies to, or at least has only been realized on, ATM datalinks.

The CSR was designed to function as the inter-LIS router in classical IP over ATM environments. The fundamental architectural intent, like that of all the approaches described in this book, is that procedures and protocols that work in the "normal" IP environment should work transparently on CSR networks. Unlike the others, however, CSR is also designed to operate in conjunction with standard ATM and classical IP over ATM subnets. It is the only approach to enable label switching devices to communicate over standard ATM VCs.

In the CSR network model, label binding follows the upstream, independent model described in Chapter 2. Upstream CSRs identify candidate IP flows that should benefit from cut-through in the network. The CSR is an example of what we have called the data-driven approach to label binding establishment. Flows are identified using source and destination addresses. The selection of flows that warrant cut-through is a matter of local configuration for each CSR. When it identifies a suitable flow, an upstream CSR determines the next hop router for a flow using normal IP routing procedures and establishes a dedicated VC for the flow toward the next hop. At transit CSRs, dedicated VCs may be spliced together to form cut-through or bypass VCs that allow the cells that constitute an IP flow to be switched at the CSR as opposed to being reassembled and processed at layer 3.

FANP is the protocol that is used both to identify the dedicated VCs between CSRs and to establish the association between individual flows and individual dedicated VCs. Individual VCs are identified in the protocol by VCID. VCID is designed to allow unique identification of VCs within a network. The VCID concept in FANP allows PVCs and SVCs in both public and private networks to be used as cut-through VCs. Flows are identified by FLOWID. The only FLOWID currently defined consists of a source/destination address pair. With respect to the association of FLOWIDs with VCIDs, FANP is a soft state protocol. This state information is cached in CSRs. If the information is not regularly refreshed, it is timed out. FANP ensures that its control messages are reliably delivered by using explicit acknowledgment. All FANP messages except PROPOSE are transmitted in IP datagrams. The PROPOSE message is transmitted directly over AAL5 on a VC.

Further work is required in some areas to fully specify the CSR architecture. For example, there are no current mechanisms defined to handle multicast and RSVP or to specify the ATM signalling parameters to be used for SVCs. Also, CSR currently does not address link types other than ATM.

In summary, the CSR proposal may have been an idea slightly ahead of its time. It is fair to acknowledge that MPLS and the label switching effort in general owe a great debt to the early work done by Toshiba. In fact, as we will see in the next chapter, the IP Switching proposal from Ipsilon, which generated so much interest in label switching, bears striking similarities to the CSR/FANP approach.

Further Reading

There are two informational RFCs on the CSR architecture:

Katsube, Y., K. Nagami, and H. Esaki. *Toshiba's Router Architecture Extensions for ATM: Overview.* RFC 2098, April 1997.

Nagami, K., et al. *Toshiba's Flow Attribute Notification Protocol (FANP) Specification.* RFC 2129, April 1997.

Toshiba also maintains an ftp site with numerous papers on the CSR at

ftp://ftp.wide.toshiba.co.jp/pub/csr/

Chapter

4

IP Switching

In this chapter we examine the label switching approach proposed by Ipsilon known as IP Switching. An individual device that implements the IP Switching architecture is, of course, an IP Switch. As noted previously, we use these terms specifically to describe the Ipsilon approach, even though they are sometimes used generically elsewhere.

IP Switching is similar in many respects to the Toshiba Cell Switching Router approach. The similarities include the use of data traffic to drive label establishment and the granularity of flows to which labels are bound. However, there are some significant differences, as we will see below. IP Switching differs from all other label switching approaches in its having been implemented in a real commercial product well in advance of the writing of this book.

One of the significant innovations of the Ipsilon approach was to define not only a label distribution protocol (which all the approaches do) but also a switch management protocol. This protocol, known as GSMP (general switch management protocol), allows an ATM switch to be controlled by an "IP Switch controller" and thus turned into an IP Switch. This protocol took the separation of control and forwarding, discussed in Section 2.1, to its logical conclusion: it enables control and forwarding to reside in separate physical boxes connected by a link, over which GSMP runs.

GSMP provides a range of technical, business, and economic benefits. In particular, at the time that Ipsilon was founded, ATM switches with capacities of around 2.5 Gbps (16 × OC-3) were becoming "commodity" items, in the sense that they were being manufactured by many vendors and were differentiated more by price than by features. In such an environment, an approach that could turn any vendor's ATM switch into something with the capabilities of a router with only a modest increase in total cost was likely to have considerable market appeal. This is exactly what GSMP enabled Ipsilon to do.

GSMP is a rather simple master/slave protocol, with the slave running on the ATM switch, and the master running on an IP Switch controller (which is really a general purpose computing engine with an ATM interface to allow it to talk to the switch). Only the slave portion has to know anything that is specific to the ATM switch hardware.

In addition to GSMP, Ipsilon also defined a label binding protocol, called Ipsilon Flow Management Protocol (IFMP), the details of which we discuss in Section 4.2. In order to spur acceptance of their approach, Ipsilon published these as Informational RFCs. Without going through a lengthy standardization process, this made the relevant specifications accessible to anyone who wanted to see them.

Having specified and published the protocol specifications, Ipsilon set about finding ATM switch vendors with whom they could form partnerships. Ipsilon would provide the IP Switch controller, some "port-ready" GSMP slave code, and engineering assistance to any interested vendor.

The open approach and the successful establishment of partnerships with many well-established switch vendors almost certainly helped speed the acceptance of IP Switching in the marketplace. For example, buying a switch from an established vendor and controlling it with software from a start-up that uses radically new protocols seems less risky than buying a complete product (with the same new protocols) from a start-up. This philosophy was apparently quite successful. The expression that seemed to be constantly applied to Ipsilon in the months following the announcement of their products was "they have gained a lot of mindshare"; that is, they had the attention of the marketplace.

We now turn to look more closely at the technology of IP Switching. We begin with an examination of the overall approach, followed by a discussion of each of the main protocols, IFMP and GSMP.

4.1 IP Switching Overview

One of the basic premises underlying the IP Switching architecture is that the alternative IP over ATM models are complex and inefficient. Recall from Chapter 1 that those models involve running two control planes: first, ATM Forum signalling and routing and then, on top of that, IP routing and address resolution. IP Switching, like other approaches described in subsequent chapters, uses just the IP component plus a label binding protocol (IFMP in this case) to allow forwarding of IP on ATM switch hardware. This approach completely removes the ATM control plane, and the need to adapt between IP and ATM control planes, from the picture.

Figure 4.1 illustrates the removal of the ATM control plane and the layers mapping between IP and ATM control planes. In Figure 4.1(a), we see the layers of control software necessary to control the ATM hardware and some of the protocols needed to map between IP and ATM control planes. Figure 4.1(b) shows a simple model of the IP Switching architecture: IP, supplemented with a label binding protocol (IFMP), directly controls the ATM hardware. Note that this figure is equally applicable to Tag Switching and ARIS.

The basic goal of IP Switching is thus to integrate ATM switches and IP routing in a simple and efficient way. A number of subgoals follow from this, including the ability to build IP routing products with high performance at relatively low cost. This in turn helps address some of the scaling issues discussed in Chapter 2. There are, however, some concerns about scalability of IP Switching, which we discuss in Chapter 7. IP Switching also aims to leverage the quality of service capabilities of ATM switches, which we address in Section 4.3.2.

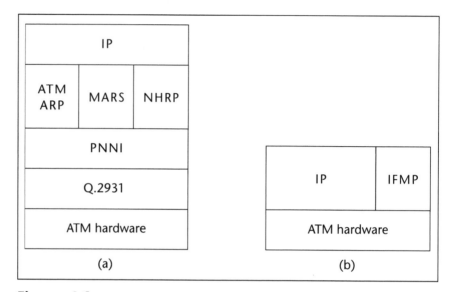

Figure 4.1   *Removing the ATM control plane: IP over Standard ATM (a); IP Switching (b).*

One consequence of removing all ATM control plane functions is that IP Switches peer directly with other IP Switches. In contrast to the CSR approach, there is no straightforward way to interconnect IP Switches using standard ATM virtual circuits. They can, however, be interconnected by virtual paths (VPs) using means discussed at the end of this section.

We begin our discussion of the IP Switching architecture by considering a single IP Switch. Figure 4.2 is a simplified illustration of the major hardware and software components of an IP Switch and of the data and control flows between switches. The switch controller is the control processor of the system. It communicates with the ATM switch itself using GSMP. Observe that the switch controller runs IP routing and forwarding code (the functions of a conventional router) as well as IFMP, GSMP, and flow classification.

Before any IP Switching can be performed, there has to be a way to get control traffic, including routing protocols and IFMP messages, between switches. A "default VC" is defined for this. It uses a well-known VCI/VPI value, so that two adjacent IP Switches will be able to communicate without first signalling for a VC. It is a VC in the sense that it connects a pair of adjacent IP Switch controllers through their attached ATM switches, but no ATM procedures (e.g., signalling) are used to establish it. Traffic that flows on the default VC is encapsulated in accordance with RFC 1483 (using LLC/SNAP, as is common for data on ATM VCs) and is sent to the switch controller and reassembled. The default VC is also used for data that does not yet have a label associated with it. Such data is forwarded in software by the switch controller.

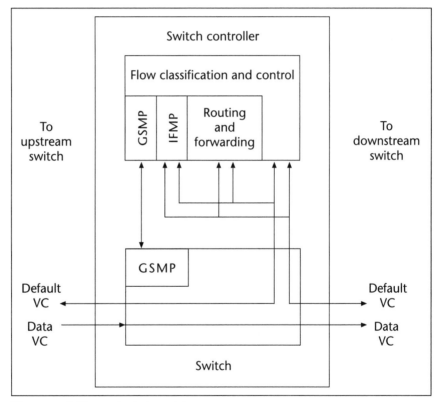

Figure 4.2 *IP Switch architecture.*

Like the other approaches we describe in this book, IP Switching relies on IP routing protocols to establish a routing information base from which the next hop for a packet can be determined. Only after this has been done, that is, only after the next hop has been identified, does the separate process of negotiating label bindings with that next hop take place.

The IFMP and GSMP modules implement the respective protocols. We have briefly discussed the role of the protocols in the introduction; they are described in more detail in Sections 4.2 and 4.3.

In very simple terms, the flow classification and control module inspects the IP traffic arriving at the switch and selects from it *flows* that are likely to benefit from being label switched. (A precise definition of a flow is provided in Section 4.2.2. For now, we can think of it as the set of packets sent from one host to another.) The module then uses IFMP to inform neighboring switches about its decisions. This ultimately enables traffic to be moved on to a label switched path, so that IP packets are forwarded by the label switching (ATM) hardware.

In common with the publicly available documentation for the other approaches described in this book, IP Switching specifies the interswitch label binding protocol (IFMP in this case) but not the internal mechanisms that use it. There are good reasons for this. Flow classification is to some extent a matter of local policy—it doesn't greatly matter if different switches use slightly different policies, although performance will certainly suffer if the policies of neighboring switches are significantly different. This is an area where a vendor can differentiate their products by providing superior capabilities to some other vendor. It is also likely that a user will want to tune these policies to match local conditions. Thus there is much less incentive to specify this part of the architecture in detail, as compared to the protocols.

While flow classification and detection approaches may not need to be specified, there are several that have been described in the literature and analyzed. One is sometimes called the *X/Y* classifier: if *X* packets matching the definition of the flow arrive in *Y* seconds, then the flow is eligible to be label switched. Another algorithm looks at TCP or UDP port numbers and tries to label switch the long-lived flows. For example, queries to the Domain Name System (DNS) are usually one or two packets long, while File Transfer Protocol (FTP) sessions tend to be much longer. Because these classification policies are local, the network administrator can select and tune the algorithms according to local conditions.

IP Switching uses the term *flow redirection*, or just *redirection*, to describe the process of binding labels to flows and establishing label switched paths. One IP Switch tells another to redirect a particular flow to it. The semantics are simply "use label *x* to send traffic from flow *y* to me." Recall that a label is just a locally significant identifier that will be used to switch some class of packets. Because IP Switching is designed to run on ATM hardware, labels represent VPI/VCI values.

If we consider a network of three IP Switches, we can see how the redirection process results in the establishment of a label switched path for a flow. In Figure 4.3 data is flowing from A via B to C on a default VC. Imagine that switch B decides that a particular flow *y* is a suitable candidate for switching. It sends a redirect to switch A specifying flow *y* and the label (VPI/VCI) on which it expects to receive it. At this point no switched path has been established through B, but A may commence sending traffic on the advertised label to B.

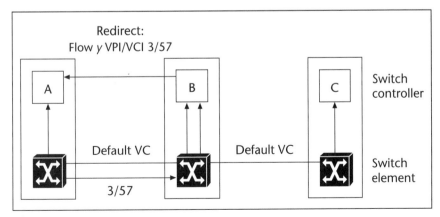

Figure 4.3 *Flow redirection. Switch B issues a* REDIRECT *message to switch A.*

When B receives data from A with this new label, it must initially forward it to C over the default VC. (Note that to prevent interleaving of packets from different flows, B must reassemble the datagrams before forwarding them.) If C then decides to issue a REDIRECT message for the flow y, the situation depicted in Figure 4.4 results. Switch B can now forward traffic on the VPI/VCI specified in the REDIRECT message from C. It can also recognize that this same flow is arriving from A on the VPI/VCI that was specified in the REDIRECT message it issued to A (see Figure 4.3). Because the same flow arrives at B on one VC and leaves on another, it now becomes possible to switch it. To do this B uses GSMP to inform its switching element to set up the appropriate switching path. In the example in Figure 4.4, B uses GSMP to set up the switch so that traffic on VPI/VCI 3/57 on the incoming port from A leaves on VPI/VCI 2/22 on the port leaving B toward C.

An important point to notice is that A and C need not necessarily be switches in this example. In the terminology of Chapter 2, they are acting as *edge* LSRs—the devices that apply the first label to a packet. An edge LSR might be implemented as a conventional router with an ATM interface to enable non-ATM (or non-IP Switching) networks to connect to an IP Switching network. Furthermore, a host with an ATM interface could apply the label to a packet, given suitable software. Thus, IP Switches can directly interconnect hosts. This is much easier to do in a data-driven model than in a control-driven one, and in fact IP Switching is the only approach to fully support host attachment at the time of writing. We return to this factor, which is certainly an advantage of IP Switching, in Chapter 7.

Again we note that there are striking similarities between IP Switching and the CSR approach of the previous chapter. The switching achieved in IP Switching following redirect looks a lot like the cut-through switching of the CSR. This reflects the fact that they are both data-driven approaches in the taxonomy of Chapter 2. Chapters 5 and 6 describe two control-driven approaches. As we discuss in Chapter 7, the distinction between control- and data-driven models is probably the most significant aspect to consider when comparing approaches.

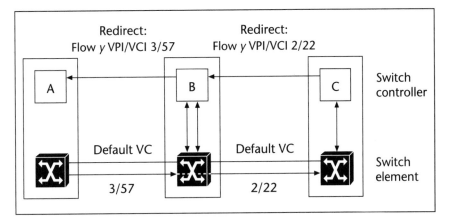

Figure 4.4 *Flow redirection and switching. Switches B and C redirect the same flow, allowing it to be switched at B.*

Although the example above showed IP Switches directly connected to each other, there is no particular reason why they could not be connected together using ATM virtual paths. This would enable them to be connected across a public ATM network that used standard ATM switches. The only requirement is that the labels used in REDIRECT messages must be contained in the VCI field, since the VPI field is used for the VP switching across the public network. This is not quite as general a solution to ATM interworking as the CSR model, which can use standard ATM switched virtual circuits (SVCs) to interconnect CSRs, but it certainly addresses part of the problem space. The other approaches in this book also use the virtual path approach to traverse standard ATM networks.

Note that each IP Switch's decision to switch a flow is made independently of the other switches and without waiting for other label bindings (REDIRECT messages) to arrive. Thus, in the taxonomy of Chapter 2, independent label binding is used. Because binding is data-driven, bindings are not piggybacked on an existing protocol, but are distributed independently. The bindings are assigned at the downstream end of a link with respect to data flow. Finally, the act of creating a binding is the result of arriving data traffic; thus, in our taxonomy, this is a data-driven approach.

4.2 Ipsilon Flow Management Protocol (IFMP)

IFMP runs on a point-to-point link between two IP Switches and is designed to communicate flow to label binding information between them. The protocol operates using the downstream label allocation model discussed in Chapter 2. Although the downstream node is in charge of label allocation and advertisement, it does so in a purely advisory way; that is, the upstream node is free to use the labels or ignore them as it sees fit. Decisions on how and when to assign labels is a matter of local policy, in the sense that each switch can make its own assignment decisions. However, it makes sense for all the switches in a domain, or at least for ones adjacent to each other, to have a coherent view of what this policy is to enable the establishment of switched paths as described above.

IFMP is a *soft state* protocol, by which we mean that the state that it installs will automatically *timeout* (i.e., be deleted after some interval) unless refreshed. In the case of IFMP, this means that flow binding information has a limited life once it is learned by an upstream switch and must be refreshed periodically as long as it is required. The messages that install flow state contain a lifetime field, which indicates for how long that state is to be considered valid. If the flow binding is not refreshed by the downstream IP Switch, it is timed out and will no longer be used by the upstream switch to forward traffic. The fact that flow information is continually refreshed by IFMP means that the protocol can run directly over IP using best effort data delivery. If a message gets lost, some flow state synchronization between two IP Switches may be temporarily lost. However, as soon as the state is refreshed (i.e., the message is resent) the flow state will again be synchronized, and all will be well. There is of course a trade-off to be made between the desire to reduce the period in which two switches might have inconsistent state and the desire to minimize the control traffic load that is generated by sending the refreshes at short intervals.

Another thing to note about the soft state approach is that there is no need to explicitly remove state information, since it will time out eventually, although an explicit removal mechanism may improve efficiency by causing faster response. Further discussion of hard state and soft state approaches appears in Chapter 7.

There are two constituent parts to IFMP, an adjacency protocol and the main redirect protocol. We discuss these in turn.

4.2.1 *IFMP's Adjacency Protocol*

Adjacency protocols are common in networking, and the name gives a good hint as to the function. Such protocols are used to communicate and discover information about immediate neighbors. They are also commonly used to make sure that a neighbor doesn't disappear silently, because of link failure or system reboot, for example, or at least to make sure a system recognizes a neighbor's reappearance.

IP Switching relies on cooperation between switches. It is important that a consistent view of the state of label assignation is maintained between switches. The IFMP adjacency protocol enables cooperating switches to exchange an initial set of information so that they acquire enough shared state to begin label exchange.

The IFMP adjacency protocol allows the switches at the ends of a link to learn each other's identity. The ADJACENCY message is encapsulated into an IP datagram and sent to the limited broadcast address. It is a convention in IP that the limited broadcast address (255.255.255.255) is listened to by all hosts on a network, and thus the IP Switches at either end of the link can send messages to each other before each knows the other's address. When an IP Switch receives an ADJACENCY message from one of its neighbors, it deduces the identity of the remote IP Switch by inspecting the source address in the IP encapsulation of the ADJACENCY message. In keeping with the soft state model, adjacency protocol messages are resent periodically.

The adjacency protocol also allows switches to agree on an instance number for the link between them and to learn the sequence number of the next message they expect to see from each other. Link instance and packet sequence numbers are used to detect loss of synchronization between two IP Switches. In the event that one switch detects some sort of error condition, the protocol enables the link to be reset: all previous flow state information learned across it is discarded, and the two parties attempt to resynchronize. In the meantime, data would be forwarded over that link using the default VC.

4.2.2 *IFMP's Redirection Protocol*

There are five message types defined in the IFMP redirection protocol. All have the common header format illustrated in Figure 4.5. All of the protocol messages are encapsulated into IP datagrams, which are sent to the unicast IP address of the peer system, learned via the IFMP adjacency protocol. The message body itself may contain more than one message element with the restriction that multiple messages, if present, must all be of the same type as indicated by the Op Code field in the header. The five message types are

- REDIRECT: The message used to bind a label to a flow and thus redirect it for switching.
- RECLAIM: Enables a label to be unbound for subsequent re-use.
- RECLAIM ACK: Acknowledgment that a RECLAIM message was received and processed.
- LABEL RANGE: Enables the acceptable range of labels for a switch to be communicated to its neighbors.
- ERROR: Used to deal with various error conditions.

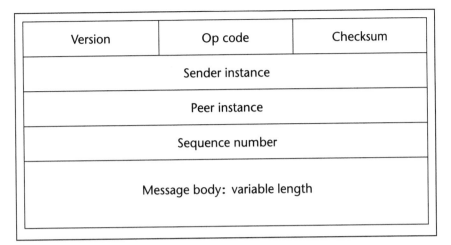

Version	Op code	Checksum
Sender instance		
Peer instance		
Sequence number		
Message body: variable length		

Figure 4.5   *IFMP* REDIRECT *protocol message format.*

The fields in the common message header are mostly self-explanatory. The purpose of instance and sequence number has already been touched upon in the description of the adjacency protocol. For example an IP Switch expects to see the sequence number in messages from its peer increase by one with each message. The sequence number is used by the redirection protocol to help process messages in order. Strict in-order processing is not always required, however. For example, if message number 2 establishes a binding between a label and a flow, and message number 1 establishes a binding between a different label and a different flow, the recipient can process them in any order.

We will confine ourselves to detailed inspection of just one message type: the REDIRECT message. (The other message formats can be found in the IFMP specification, RFC 1953.) We focus on REDIRECT not just because it is so central to IP Switching but also because it introduces in a concrete way something that we have glossed over until now, the precise definition of a flow.

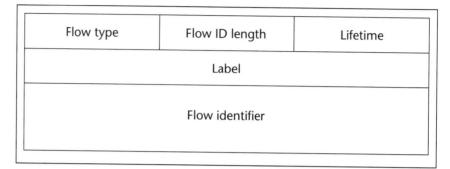

Flow type	Flow ID length	Lifetime
Label		
Flow identifier		

Figure 4.6   *IFMP* REDIRECT *message body.*

The REDIRECT message body format is illustrated in Figure 4.6. Looking at the message we see *flow type* and *flow identifier* for the first time. At this point in our discussion of IP Switching, the general term *flow*, which has sufficed in our description up until now, will no longer do. Flow identifiers in IP Switching are a little more complicated than a general familiarity with label switching concepts might lead us to expect.

An IP *flow* is often understood to refer to a sequence of datagrams from one source IP address to another destination IP address. Such a flow, which we can call a host-to-host flow, can be described or identified by an ordered pair of the form <source address, destination address>. Roughly speaking, this is called a Type 2 flow in IP Switching. We can also specify a flow at a finer granularity by including transport layer port addresses, so the flow would be identified by <source address, source port, destination address, destination port>. This enables different applications between the same pair of machines to be distinguished. Ipsilon calls these Type 1 flows. These flow definitions are fairly common; for example, the Resource Reservation Protocol (RSVP) uses similar definitions. Ipsilon's definitions of flows build on these but also include a number of other fields from the IP datagram header in the flow identifier. The reason for including these fields will become clear as we discuss the usage of flow identifiers.

The IP Switching architecture allows for a variety of flow types to be defined, and there are two such types at the time of writing.

The formats of the Type 1 and Type 2 flow identifiers are illustrated in Figure 4.7 and Figure 4.8, respectively.

The flow Type 1 identifier is used to identify application flows and thus includes the source and destination protocol port numbers. In addition, it includes five fields from the IP version 4 (IPv4) header. These are the version, the IP header length (IHL), the type of service byte (TOS), the time-to-live field (TTL), and the protocol ID. The meanings of these fields is not particularly important at this point; we simply note that they are exact replicas of fields in the IPv4 header. Note also that at a given point in the network, these fields should remain constant for all the packets belonging to the same application flow. The precise definition of a flow is simply this: a set of packets that have the same value in all the header fields is included in the corresponding flow identifier.

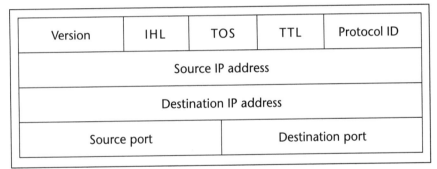

Figure 4.7 *IFMP flow Type 1 identifier.*

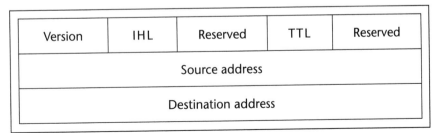

Figure 4.8 *IFMP flow Type 2 identifier.*

The flow Type 2 identifier corresponds to the host-to-host flow mentioned above. It includes all the same fields from the IPv4 header as a Type 1 identifier except for the protocol number and TOS byte. The reason to exclude these fields is that they are not likely to be the same for all packets between a pair of hosts.

The apparent complexity of these flow types when compared with the simple model just described or with those used by the CSR arises from two capabilities provided by the IP Switching architecture. As we will see in Section 4.2.5, it handles TTL "correctly"; it also provides some protection against *spoofing*. Spoofing is a general term for a number of techniques used for gaining unauthorized access to network or computer resources. Label switching offers some particular opportunities for spoofing attacks. The IP Switching architecture includes some features to make such attacks more difficult. The flow identifiers are only one component involved in providing this anti-spoofing protection. The other is the encapsulation used on the redirected VCs. We will examine this first and will return to the issue of spoofing in Section 4.2.4.

4.2.3 *Encapsulation of Redirected Flows*

In our discussion of redirection in Section 4.1 we glossed over the details of encapsulation, that is, the representation of IP packets on redirected VCs. A significant detail is that when data is sent on a redirected VC the encapsulation is changed from the one used on the default VC. Figure 4.9 illustrates the encapsulations used on both default and redirected VCs for Type 2 flows. We will consider the simpler case of Type 2 flows in detail before explaining the slight differences when Type 1 flows are used.

The important differences between the two encapsulations are that when a flow is moved onto its own redirected VC from the default VC

- The LLC and SNAP fields disappear.
- The IP header gets transformed into an IFMP flow type header. (With Type 1 flows, the TCP or UDP header would also be affected, for reasons explained below.)

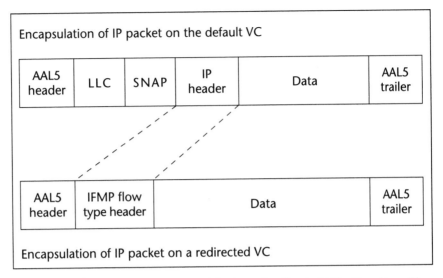

Figure 4.9   *Encapsulation on default and redirected VCs (flow Type 2).*

The disappearance of the LLC/SNAP fields is not very significant, as they were not doing much apart from indicating that the layer 3 protocol is IP. What happens in transforming the IP and TCP/UDP headers is more complex and interesting. The header is actually compressed, in that some fields are removed. It should be apparent that such a compression process needs to be reversible.

Figure 4.10 illustrates the transformation in more detail. The figure shows a standard IPv4 header, a flow Type 2 identifier, and the encapsulation (or header) used for datagrams of flow Type 2 on a redirected VC. In addition to the fields described above, the IPv4 header contains

- Total length of the datagram
- Identification, flags, and fragment offset, which are used for IP fragmentation
- A header checksum, used to check for corruption of the header

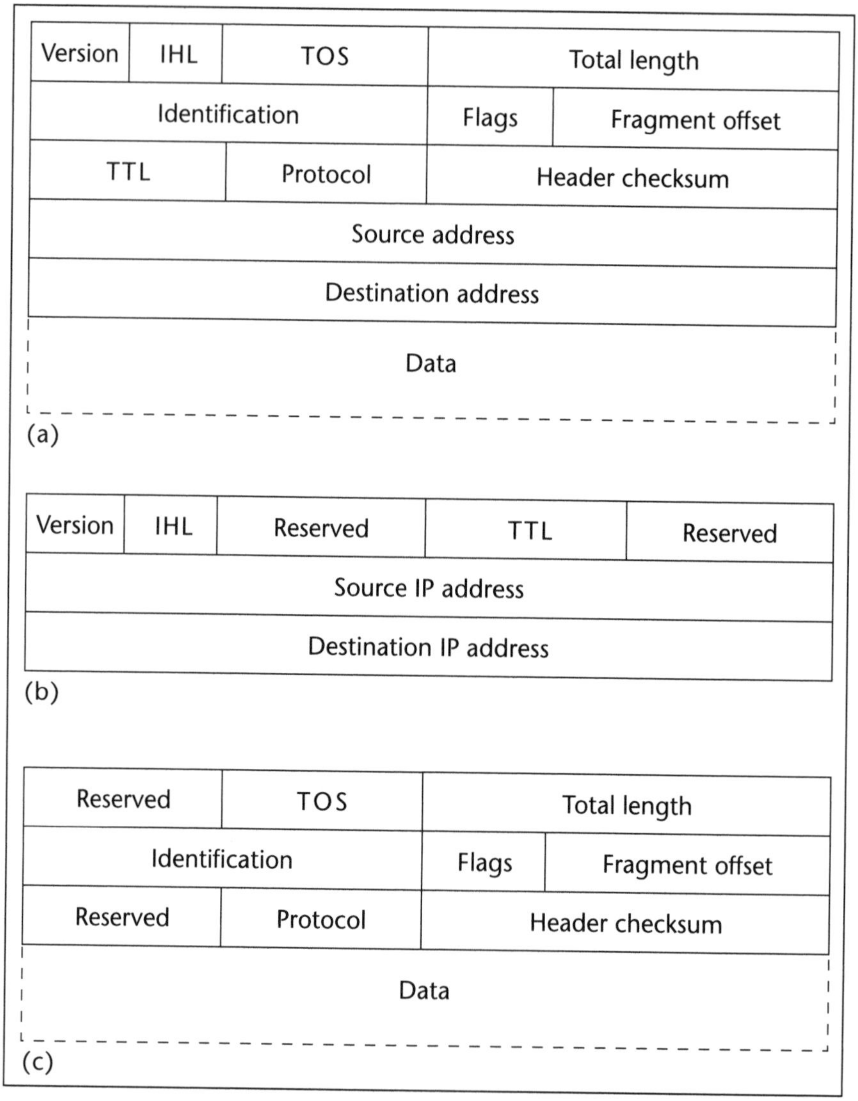

Version	IHL	TOS	Total length	
Identification		Flags	Fragment offset
TTL	Protocol	Header checksum	
Source address			
Destination address			
Data			

(a)

Version	IHL	Reserved	TTL	Reserved
Source IP address				
Destination IP address				

(b)

Reserved	TOS	Total length	
Identification		Flags	Fragment offset
Reserved	Protocol	Header checksum	
Data			

(c)

Figure 4.10 *IPv4 header compression: IPv4 header (a); IFMP flow Type 2 identifier (b); and flow Type 2 encapsulation (c). The flow identifier and flow encapsulation together contain all the fields of the IP header.*

Note that all of these fields appear in the flow Type 2 encapsulation, along with the type of service field and the protocol number. Every other field from the IP header is included in the flow Type 2 identifier. That is, given a flow identifier and the matching flow encapsulation, all the fields of the original IP header can be reconstructed. Using the labels of the three parts of Figure 4.10, we observe that a = b + c. We now examine how this works in practice.

Recall that the sequence of events leading up to the appearance of a redirected flow on a certain VC is as follows:

1. An IP Switch selects a flow by inspection of its IP header (Figure 4.10a).

2. The switch sends a REDIRECT message containing a flow identifier (Figure 4.10b) and a VCI/VPI to use for the selected flow to its upstream neighbor.

3. The upstream IP Switch sends the flow on the VC specified in the REDIRECT message using the appropriate flow type encapsulation. In this case it is flow Type 2 (Figure 4.10c).

Now consider an IP Switch receiving a redirected flow. The flow arrives on the VPI/VCI, which the switch selected and communicated to its upstream neighbor using a REDIRECT message. The switch keeps a copy of all REDIRECT messages it has sent. Thus it can use the VPI/VCI of the incoming flow to obtain the corresponding flow identifier. Now it has both the flow identifier and the arriving flow itself. As we observed, it is possible to generate the original IPv4 header by combining these two together.

Almost identical mechanisms to those described above are used for flow Type 1. One difference is that now the flow identifier contains the TOS and protocol fields, which means that they don't need to be included in the encapsulation. Also, because the flow identifier includes the source and destination port numbers from the TCP or UDP header, these fields are also removed from the packet before transmission. The reconstruction of the original headers—now including TCP or UDP as well as IP—is performed as before, again relying on the fact that the flow identifier and encapsulated packet together provide everything that is needed to recreate the original packet headers.

There are two fields that require a little extra attention for both flow types. These are the TTL, which needs to be decremented at the end of a label switched path, and the header checksum, which needs to be updated as a result of the change to the TTL. The details of handling these fields are discussed in Section 4.2.5.

Although compression is usually employed to reduce bandwidth utilization, in this case the removal of fields from the packet and reconstruction of those fields at the end of a switched path offers an additional (and perhaps more important) benefit, which is protection against spoofing. We note that the ability to perform compression directly follows from the fine-grained nature of flows. Because many fields in the IP header are the same for all packets in a flow, we can send those fields once—in the flow identifier, rather than sending them in every packet. If flow identifiers were more coarse-grained, representing, say, all traffic to a certain destination prefix, then it would not be possible to remove fields from the IP header.

4.2.4   *IFMP and Security*

Consider the general label switching paradigm where a label switching router obtains a label and the definition of the corresponding forwarding equivalence class (an FEC, as defined in Chapter 2) from its next hop for that FEC. It is then capable of forwarding traffic belonging to that FEC using the label. At the next hop label switch, only the label is used in deciding how to further forward the traffic. What happens if the upstream node uses the label incorrectly to forward packets that do not belong to the FEC? It may help to rephrase this in the more familiar terms of destination address-based forwarding. If a switch says to a peer "send me traffic for address 171.69.210.139 using label y," then what happens if the peer sends packets addressed to 155.3.21.139 using this label? The simple answer is that they will get sent along the wrong label switched path. What happens beyond that—that is, what the effect of the packets traveling on the wrong path is—is a much harder question to answer. The result may simply be an annoying lack of connectivity. It is also possible that the filtering rules that might have prevented packets from passing through a certain point in the network might be violated. This would certainly be undesirable.

The IP header regeneration operation described in the previous section makes this kind of mistake (or attack), and others like it, more difficult. The IP address fields are under the "control" of the receiving system. Unless the receiving system at the end of the IP Switched path is compromised, it will regenerate a packet addressed to the correct system (for that VC) with a source address that matches the flow ID.

This feature of IP Switching clearly helps mitigate the effects of one form of operational error or deliberate attack. There are undoubtedly many that it will not catch. However, this feature is a capability that none of the other label switching schemes possess. The fact that only IP Switching has this capability reflects both an attention to detail in bringing the product to market, as well as a focus on particular deployment scenarios. For example, this type of attack could not be launched on an Internet service provider using label switching only within its backbone. We return to this issue in Chapter 7.

4.2.5 *IFMP and TTL*

Recall from Chapter 2 that time-to-live (TTL) is used to mitigate the effects of loops. The TTL field is part of the IP header and can be processed by a conventional router. In fact, it is a requirement that IP routers process this field, decrementing it by one before they forward a packet and discarding the packet if the TTL becomes zero after the decrement operation. The IP TTL cannot be processed by an ATM switch; as a cell switch it is only capable of operating on fields in the ATM cell header. An IP Switch, which uses an ATM switch to forward label switched IP packets, can therefore not decrement TTL at every hop. However, IP Switching does manage to decrement TTL at the end of a label switched path and to mitigate the effect of loops, using some mechanisms that we now examine.

IP Switching ensures that the TTL field in an IP datagram at the end of an IP Switched path contains the same value it would have had if it had passed through a path of conventional routers with the same number of hops. In simple terms, what happens is that the IP TTL is removed from the IP datagram at the start of an IP Switched path, and a new TTL value is decremented by the number of IP Switch hops the packet has traversed and is inserted at the end of the path. Note the difference between this case and the conventional one: although the TTL is correct at the *end* of the IP Switched path, that "correctness" is achieved by a mechanism that is different from the decrement at each hop required of routers.

If we look again at the flow identifiers in Figures 4.7 and 4.8, we see that they contain a TTL field. The value in this field is copied from the header of an IP datagram that an IP Switch has selected for redirection. A REDIRECT message for the datagram contains both a label and a flow identifier. In Figure 4.11 we see switch B part way through setting up a switched flow. Switch B has already elected to redirect the flow *y*. It has sent a REDIRECT message to A saying "redirect flow *y* to me on VPI/VCI 3/57." As part of the flow identifier, B has specified that the TTL for packets eligible to be sent on the redirected circuit is *n*.

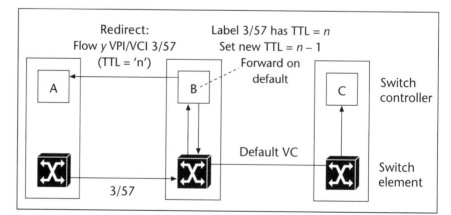

Figure 4.11   *TTL handling in switched flow setup.*

Now suppose that switch C has not yet elected to redirect the flow. Switch B must, therefore, forward the flow y, now arriving on 3/57, on the default VC. To do this B uses the flow label (3/57) to obtain the flow identifier record and from that obtains the IPv4 header information that would normally be in the packets that constitute flow y at this point. The TTL is part of this information. Switch B regenerates the header by combining the flow encapsulation and flow identifier in the manner we discussed previously (see Section 4.2.3 and Figure 4.10). Switch B now performs the normal router forwarding procedures on this packet including decrementing the TTL. The new TTL is set to $n - 1$, as shown in the figure, and the packet is forwarded on the default VC toward C. Now if C were to select this same flow for redirection, it would include the TTL of $n - 1$ in the flow identifier. Once redirection had taken place, C would insert the value $n - 1$ in the TTL field and process the packet. Thus it should be clear that, for a label switched path of any length, the TTL placed in the packet at the end will be the correct one, based on the number of hops in the path.

An interesting side effect of the inclusion of TTL in the flow identifier is that all the packets going down a label switched path must have exactly the same TTL. Because the flow identifier already restricts the packets of a flow to be from the same host, and because the host almost certainly puts the same TTL value in every packet it sends (unless it is running some diagnostic tool such as traceroute), this is not really a big restriction. It does mean that if a routing change between the sending host and the start of the label switched path changes the number of hops the packets go through, then the established label switched path will become useless. This is likely to be a rare occurrence in a healthy network. It is also worth noting that, if some new flow type were defined that was less fine-grained than host-to-host flows, some other means of dealing with TTL would be needed.

By decrementing TTL correctly from one end of a label switched path to the other, the mechanism just described ensures that, if a forwarding loop that includes both IP Switches and conventional routers develops, looping packets will be discarded when their TTL reaches zero. If the loop was purely among IP Switches, then the worst that can happen is a label switched "spiral" would form, ending at the IP Switch that was receiving packets with TTL = 1. This last IP Switch would discard the packets as their TTL expired and thus would never be able to set up a switched path to the next hop. This is illustrated in Figure 4.12. The spiral would of course be resolved when routing reconverged to break the loop. Note that this spiral is the same one that packets would follow if normal IP routing were used, but in the IP Switching case packets get to the end of the spiral without having their TTL decremented by one at every hop. The crucial fact is that packets do not loop *infinitely*, which would be possible in a label switching scheme that did not somehow deal with TTL. (All schemes in this book except the CSR have mechanisms to prevent infinite loops. CSR will need to develop such a mechanism to be practically useful—perhaps it already has, but the public specifications fail to reveal it.) Note that in the taxonomy of Chapter 2, this is a loop mitigation scheme, not a loop prevention scheme.

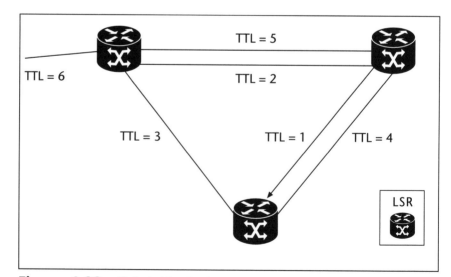

Figure 4.12   *IP Switching in the presence of a routing loop. In the worst case, a label switched spiral forms, terminating at the IP Switch that receives packets with TTL = 1.*

We mentioned in Section 4.2.3 that header fields were copied from the IPv4 header into the flow encapsulation used on the redirected VC or into the flow identifier. One field, however, is treated in a slightly different way. The IPv4 header checksum is, as its name implies, a checksum over all the data in the IPv4 header. Because the TTL is modified at the downstream end of the label switched path, it follows that the checksum must be as well. It is possible to recalculate it, as all the data needed to do so is present. However, this would mask any corruption of the header that might have happened up to the point of recalculation, either on the label switched path or before it. So instead, at the start of a switched path, the value of the TTL is subtracted from the value of the header checksum and the result is sent in the encapsulation. The switch at the end of the path only has to add the value that it inserts in the TTL field to the value of the header checksum in the encapsulation to regenerate the correct IPv4 checksum. This is the exact checksum that would have been in the packet if it had been transmitted by a sequence of conventional routers.

4.3 General Switch Management Protocol (GSMP)

We provide an introduction to the GSMP because it is part of the overall IP Switching architecture. However, it is important to realize that, from a technology perspective, IP Switching is essentially independent of GSMP, and vice versa. GSMP is used solely to control an ATM switch and the VC connections made across it. We could make an IP Switch without using GSMP. Also, one can use GSMP to control ATM switches without building an IP Switch. For example, one could build a controller that implemented standard ATM signalling (e.g., Q.2931) and controlled a switch using GSMP.

It is not technologically necessary to run a protocol between an external controller and a switch—one could just write custom switch control software for each different ATM switch. However, as noted at the start of this chapter, such an approach is not efficient if the goal is to support IP Switching on multiple switch platforms. The same argument does not hold with the Ipsilon Flow Management Protocol (IFMP). Because IP Switching requires cooperation between peers, a standard protocol is needed to transport flow information between them. It makes no sense to consider building an IP Switch without defining the interswitch protocol. Thus, we make a distinction between the two protocols: IFMP is clearly a key architectural component of IP Switching, whereas GSMP is more an implementation optimization.

The GSMP is a master/slave protocol where an ATM switch is the slave. The protocol specifies that the master and slave are connected via an ATM link. The master could be any general purpose computer (and in Ipsilon's products is actually an Intel-based PC). The specification describes the protocol as being one for "general purpose ATM switch control." The protocol allows the master to

- Establish and release VC connections across the switch
- Add and delete leaves to point to multipoint connections
- Perform port management (Up, Down, Reset, Loopback)
- Request data (configuration information, statistics)

In addition the protocol allows the slave to inform the master if something interesting, such as a link failure, happens on the switch.

As with IFMP, GSMP has an adjacency part and a connection management part, and we will consider each in turn. Before doing that we will look briefly at the GSMP packet format illustrated in Figure 4.13, because it is common to both parts of the protocol. GSMP packets are LLC/SNAP encapsulated and sent over an ATM link using AAL5. This is a common encapsulation for data sent over ATM links (see RFC 1483). The LLC/SNAP encapsulation allows other packets (from different protocols) to be sent on the link at the same time and be distinguished from the GSMP packets at the receiver. The actual values in the LLC and SNAP fields together identify that the protocol thus encapsulated is GSMP.

LLC (0xAA 0xAA 0x03)	SNAP
SNAP (0x00 0x00 0x00 0x88 0x0C)	
GSMP message	
Pad and AAL5 trailer	

Figure 4.13 *GSMP packet format.*

Note that GSMP messages, unlike IFMP messages, are not sent as IP packets. They are sent directly inside the LLC/SNAP encapsulation. This reflects the fact that GSMP is used to control a node that is assumed to know nothing about IP—an ATM switch—whereas IFMP is a peer-to-peer protocol between a pair of IP-capable nodes.

4.3.1 *GSMP Adjacency Protocol*

We have already discussed the general purpose behind adjacency protocols—to provide some initial information to the communicating parties before they begin their "real" work. It is not surprising that the GSMP and IFMP adjacency protocols are quite similar. The GSMP adjacency protocol message format is illustrated in Figure 4.14. The sender and receiver names contain a number that identifies the switches. The field is long enough to accommodate a standard MAC address. This is convenient because most hardware has one of these and MAC addresses are assigned to ensure that they are globally unique; this makes it easier to manage networks of machines than might otherwise be the case.

The port numbers are locally assigned numbers for the link between the sender and the receiver. The instance field is used in the manner that we discussed previously for IFMP and is changed if a loss of synchronization between sender and receiver occurs, so that old messages can be ignored. In fact, all the fields are used in a way semantically equivalent to those in the IFMP adjacency protocol. They are used initially to gain information about the system at the other end of the link and then to monitor the links status. For example, if sender port or name were to change from one message to another, then clearly some remedial action would be called for (in this case resetting the link).

4.3.2 *GSMP Connection Management Protocol*

All the connection management messages, with the exception of MOVE BRANCH, have the same format. The master can set a field that indicates to the slave whether it requires a response. Responses are only provided if requested. The format of the connection management messages is shown in Figure 4.15. The names of most of the fields are fairly self-explanatory. There are two fields that are worthy of further comment: port session number and priority.

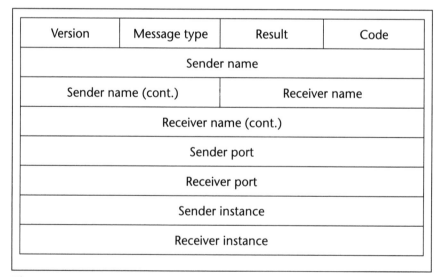

Figure 4.14   *GSMP adjacency protocol message.*

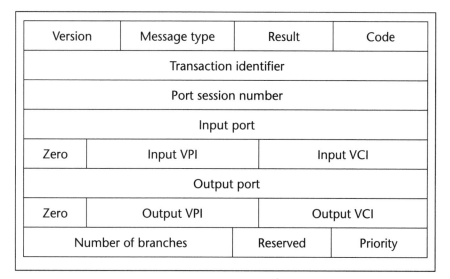

Figure 4.15 *GSMP connection management message format.*

The port session number is used to ensure consistency between the GSMP master and slave. If a port on a switch goes out of service and is restored, its port session number must change, and the GSMP master will be unable to control that port until it learns the new port session number. This enables the master to reestablish state that may have been lost while the port was out of service.

Note that in this message there is only one "port session number" field, even though a connection involves two ports. This is because GSMP associates connection state with an input port, implying that GSMP does not need to know if an output port has gone down and come back up. In the event that this happens, the switch is required to reestablish any lost connections.

The other field of interest is priority. A great part of the complexity of ATM switch hardware and ATM signalling software is involved with quality of service (QOS). By contrast, the IP Switching approach as originally specified had very little to say about QOS. The simple priority field in GSMP provides a basic capability to use priority-based queuing at an output port.

Simple priority queuing is not the same as the more powerful and complex techniques available from ATM cell switching, but it may be that it is adequate for switching IP flows, given the lack of QOS mechanisms generally available to IP traffic today. It is not specified how these priorities are to be set, but one possible way is to do so based on the state of the precedence bits in the IP Type of Service field.

Some of the research papers produced by Ipsilon and some of their partners suggest ways in which the queuing, scheduling, and traffic management capabilities of ATM hardware could be exploited in combination with RSVP (among other mechanisms) to provide QOS capabilities for IP flows. This is certainly possible but not with GSMP as specified in RFC 1987. However, QOS extensions to GSMP are underway at the time of writing, and some references are provided in the Bibliography. Certainly the fact that IP Switching allows each application flow to have its own VC, coupled with the fact that many ATM switches can provide sophisticated per-VC queuing capabilities, suggests that significant QOS capabilities may be provided by this approach.

Another interesting feature of the protocol when compared with ATM signalling is that it makes no distinction between unicast and multicast connections. There is, for example, a single ADD BRANCH message. Whether it means "make a unicast connection" or "add this branch to an existing connection" is determined by the slave and depends on the context existing at the time the message is received. If the specified port already has a connection from the specified input VPI/VCI to another output connection, a new branch will be added. If there is no connection, then one will be established.

As mentioned earlier, GSMP also contains some messages for statistics gathering, for example, counts of the number of cells transmitted on a VC, and general port and switch management. These capabilities are not really central to the theme of this book and so we do not deal with them here. The GSMP specification, RFC 1987, describes these details.

4.4 Implementations

IP Switching products have been available since 1996. The Ipsilon product family uses an Intel Pentium-based PC running a highly modified version of Free BSD (UNIX) as the switch controller. Ipsilon also offers a number of ATM switches that are controlled by the switch controller, which attaches to one port of the switch. In addition to ATM-only switches, there are a number of edge devices that allow Ethernet and FDDI LANs to be connected to an IP Switching backbone. Note that these latter devices always function as edge LSRs, as defined in Chapter 2. Ipsilon has also put some effort into providing ATM network interface device drivers that allow hosts to connect directly to an IP Switching backbone.

Ipsilon also established partnerships with a considerable number of switch vendors. These partners implemented GSMP, and thus it is possible to buy an IP Switch controller from Ipsilon—a PC with Ipsilon software and an ATM interface—and an ATM switch from an established switch vendor. The result is a fully functional IP Switch.

One question that arises in the context of implementation concerns the performance of IP Switching. The references in the Further Reading section of this chapter give some insight on this issue, and we discuss the performance of IP Switching as compared to other approaches in Chapter 7.

4.5 Summary

IP Switching is a data-driven approach to label switching specified for use over ATM hardware and links. It was invented soon after CSR but has a significantly different attitude toward ATM. Unlike CSR, it is not designed to allow label switches to communicate over standard VCs. It does, however, address some of the problems encountered when using ATM switch hardware to forward IP packets.

The IP Switching approach has made many major contributions to the label switching effort. Although is was not the first approach invented, it was the first that delivered real products and caused the flurry of activity that resulted in the development of Tag Switching and, ultimately, the formation of the MPLS working group in the IETF.

In addition to IFMP, the label binding protocol, IP Switching contributed GSMP, a useful general purpose technique for controlling ATM switches with third-party software, thus enabling a large number of vendors' switches to easily become IP Switches. GSMP may also be used by any other software that can control an ATM switch, for example, software to support standard ATM signalling.

Alone among label switching approaches, IP Switching offers some protection against the dangers of incorrect flows being submitted on a label switched path. It is also unique in enabling label switched paths to extend all the way to hosts, provided they have ATM interfaces and suitable software.

Further Reading

There is a wealth of interesting information on IP Switching at Ipsilon's Website at

   www.ipsilon.com

The three informational RFCs (1953, 1954, 1987) that describe the protocols and the transmission of flow labeled IPv4 on ATM datalinks are available there. In addition, some excellent papers that treat IP Switching in more depth are available at

   ftp://ds.internic.net/rfc

Publications that cover IP Switching include

Lin, S., and N. McKeown. "A Simulation Study of IP Switching." In Proceedings of the ACM SIGCOMM 97, Cannes, France, September 1997.

Newman, P., T. Lyon, and G. Minshall. "Flow Labeled IP: A Connectionless Approach to ATM." In Proceedings of the IEEE Infocom, March 1996.

Newman, P., T. Lyon, and G. Minshall. "IP Switching: ATM Under IP."
IEEE/ACM Transactions on Networking. Forthcoming.

Newman, P., G. Minshall, T. Lyon, and L. Huston. "IP Switching and
Gigabit Routers." *IEEE Communications Magazine* January 1997.

QOS extensions to GSMP are discussed in

www.ipsilon.com/~pn/gsmp/gsmp-qos-draft01.txt

The standard reference for encapsulation of network layer traffic over ATM is RFC 1483, available at

ftp://ds.internic.net/rfc

Chapter

5

Tag Switching

In this chapter we look at Tag Switching. We begin with an overview of the Tag Switching design goals and how it provides a variety of different functions. These include destination-based routing, hierarchy of routing knowledge, multicast, and explicit routes. Following this, we describe possible alternatives for carrying tag information in packets. Unlike the approaches described so far, Tag Switching is not restricted to running only on ATM hardware. In fact, there are some special procedures required to cover the case of ATM. We conclude this chapter with a brief overview of the main new protocol that Tag Switching requires, the Tag Distribution Protocol (TDP).

Like all the approaches described in this book, Tag Switching has its own terminology. A router that supports Tag Switching is called a Tag Switching Router (TSR). Labels are called *tags* (which is why the scheme is called "Tag Switching"). Instead of incoming label we'll use *incoming tag*, and instead of outgoing label we'll use *outgoing tag*. A label switching forwarding table is called a *Tag Forwarding Information Base* (TFIB).

The material in this chapter is largely based on the publicly available documents on Tag Switching, primarily a number of Internet drafts. More details are provided in the Further Reading section at the end of this chapter.

5.1 Tag Switching Overview

In Chapter 1 we saw that there were many motivations behind the development of the various label switching approaches, such as additional routing functionality, improved scalability of the routing system, better forwarding performance, and more flexibility of the routing system. However, the one that has been most widely appreciated is the easiest to understand: performance. The idea is simple: provide the functionality of a router (IP forwarding) with the performance (and cost) of an ATM switch.

The design goals of Tag Switching are rather broad. In particular, Tag Switching has focused on adding functionality (such as explicit routes) and improving scalability (e.g., through the use of a hierarchy of routing knowledge), as the following sections will illustrate. Moreover, Tag Switching aims at being link layer independent, thus allowing operation over virtually any media type, not just ATM. High performance is just one among many goals for Tag Switching.

Tag Switching can be implemented in a variety of devices, such as routers or ATM switches. Implementing Tag Switching on routers doesn't require hardware modifications to the routers, although one certainly could provide specialized hardware support for high performance Tag Switching forwarding. Implementing Tag Switching on ATM switches doesn't require any modifications to the hardware used by these switches (although Tag Switching could benefit from certain hardware modifications, as we'll describe below); support for Tag Switching on ATM switches can be achieved purely by upgrading software.

A Tag Switching network consists of Tag Edge Routers, and Tag Switching Routers (TSRs). The role of Tag Edge Routers is to turn untagged packets into tagged packets, and vice versa. The role of TSRs is to forward tagged packets. In the terminology of Chapter 2, Tag Edge Routers are the Edge Label Switching Routers (Edge LSRs) and TSRs are equivalent to LSRs.

5.1.1 *Support for Destination-Based Routing*

In the other approaches we have seen so far, destination-based routing—the ability to deliver a packet to its IP destination using label switching—is really the only capability provided. In Tag Switching (and in ARIS, as we will see later), it is one function of many. It is, however, the fundamental capability that any approach must provide.

Recall that, in the context of destination-based routing, a Forwarding Equivalence Class (FEC) is associated with an address prefix. Using the information provided by unicast routing protocols (e.g., OSPF, RIP, BGP) a conventional router constructs mappings between FECs (address prefixes) and their corresponding next hops and uses this mapping for the actual packet forwarding.

To support destination-based routing, a TSR, just like an ordinary router, participates in unicast routing protocols and uses the information provided by these protocols to construct its mapping between FECs (expressed as address prefixes) and their corresponding next hops. However, in contrast with an ordinary router, a TSR doesn't use this mapping for the actual packet forwarding—this mapping is used by the Tag Switching control component only for the purpose of constructing its Tag Forwarding Information Base (TFIB); the TFIB is used for the actual packet forwarding.

Once a TSR has constructed a mapping between a particular FEC and its next hop, the TSR is ready to construct an entry in its TFIB. The information needed to construct the entry is provided from three sources:

1. A local binding between the FEC and a tag

2. A mapping between the FEC and the next hop for that FEC (provided by the routing protocol(s) running on the TSR)

3. A remote binding between the FEC and a tag that is received from the next hop

To create a local binding for a particular FEC, the TSR takes a tag from its pool of free tags and updates its TFIB as follows. The TSR uses the tag as an index in its TFIB to determine a particular TFIB entry that has to be updated. Once the entry is determined, the incoming tag in that entry is set to the tag that the TSR took from the pool of free tags, the next hop in the entry is set to the address of the next hop associated with the FEC, and the outgoing interface is set to the interface that should be used to reach the next hop. Note that the local binding procedure relies on the information provided by the routing protocols to determine the next hop and the outgoing interface for a particular FEC (address prefix). Therefore, the existence of the FEC to next hop mapping is a prerequisite for creating a local binding.

Once a TSR creates a local binding, it is ready to distribute the information about this binding to other TSRs. The binding information that a TSR distributes to other TSRs consists of a set of tuples <address prefix, tag>, where *address prefix* identifies a particular FEC, and *tag* defines the tag value that the TSR uses for its local binding associated with the FEC.

When a TSR has completed its local binding, the only missing information in the TFIB entry is the outgoing tag. The TSR obtains this information from the tag binding information distributed by other TSRs. When a TSR receives tag binding information from another TSR, the TSR proceeds as follows. First the TSR checks for the presence of its local binding for the FEC carried as part of the received tag binding information. If the local binding is present, the TSR checks whether the information was received from the TSR that is the next hop for the FEC. If it has, then the TSR locates an entry in its TFIB that contains the binding for that FEC and updates the outgoing tag of that entry with the tag from the received binding information. At this point the TFIB entry is completely populated and could be used for packet forwarding.

If the TSR receives tag binding information from another TSR, but the TSR doesn't have a local binding for the FEC carried as part of the received binding information, the TSR has two options. The first one is to keep this information, in case the TSR is able to use it later (if the local binding is created at some later point). The second option is to discard the binding information. Of course, if the TSR decides to use the second option, the TSR should be able to ask the other TSR to resend the tag binding information, which in turn places certain requirements on the mechanism(s) used to distribute tag binding information. The same two options apply when the TSR receives tag binding information from another TSR and the TSR has a local binding for the FEC carried as part of the received binding information, but the next hop contained in the local binding is different from the TSR from whom the information was received.

The specific mechanisms for distributing tag binding information depend on the routing protocol that the TSR uses for constructing its FEC to next hop mapping. If the mapping is constructed via link-state routing protocols (e.g., OSPF), the distribution of tag binding information is provided via a separate protocol, called the Tag Distribution Protocol (TDP). The reason for this is that with link-state routing protocols, routing information is flooded unmodified among a set of (not necessarily adjacent) routers participating in a protocol, whereas the tag binding information is usually distributed only among adjacent routers. This makes link-state routing protocols not well suited for piggybacking tag binding information. Thus, one might imagine that tag bindings could be piggybacked on a distance vector protocol such as RIP. In fact, even if the routing protocol used is RIP or RIP-II, the distribution of tag binding information is provided via TDP as well. The reason for this is that it would be fairly hard (if not impossible) to modify these protocols in a backward-compatible fashion to allow piggybacking of tag binding information. However, when the mapping is constructed via BGP, the tag binding information could be piggybacked on top of BGP as a separate BGP attribute. This is because BGP distributes information about address prefixes (FECs) and is extensible enough to allow piggybacking in a backward-compatible way.

In order for a TSR to distribute tag binding information, the TSR has to know the set of other TSRs to whom this information must be distributed. The TSR constructs this set by using the information provided by the routing protocol(s) running on the TSR. The TSR includes in this set every TSR with whom the TSR maintains a routing peer relationship. Note that usually this results in a situation where the set includes all the TSRs that share a common subnetwork with at least one of the interfaces of the local TSR.

However, as we'll see in the following section, there are some exceptions.

To illustrate how Tag Switching supports destination-based forwarding consider an example shown in Figure 5.1. Assume that there is a set of destinations (expressed as an address prefix 192.6/16[1]) that are directly connected to TSR E, and further assume that in a steady state (when all the links are operational) both TSR B and TSR D use TSR E as the next hop for the FEC associated with 192.6/16, TSR A uses TSR B as its next hop for this FEC, and TSR C uses TSR D as its next hop for this FEC. Each TSR has three interfaces, labeled if0, if1, and if2. For the purpose of this example it is irrelevant whether these interfaces correspond to point-to-point or multiaccess (e.g., Ethernet) subnetworks. It also does not matter what routing protocol was used to determine the next hops. In this example we also assume that all the TSRs maintain their TFIBs, as well as their pools of free tags, on a per-TSR (rather than on a per-interface) basis.

First consider how all the TSRs construct their TFIBs. As soon as TSR A determines the next hop (TSR B) for the FEC associated with 192.6/16, TSR A takes a tag from its pool of free tags. Let's assume that the value of this tag is 100. TSR A uses this tag as an index in its TFIB to find an entry that should be updated. Once the entry is found, A sets the incoming tag of this entry to 100, the next hop to B, and the outgoing interface to if1. As soon as B determines the next hop (TSR E) for the FEC associated with 192.6/16, TSR B takes a tag from its pool of free tags. Let's assume that the value of this tag is 6. TSR B uses this tag as an index in its TFIB to find an entry that should be updated. Once the entry is found, A sets the incoming tag of this entry to 6, the next hop to E, and the outgoing interface to if1. TSRs C and D use similar procedures to create their local bindings.

---

[1] We use the notation *A.B/y* to indicate an address prefix and its length in bits (*y*). Prefixes in an IP version 4 routing table can be of various lengths up to 32 bits.

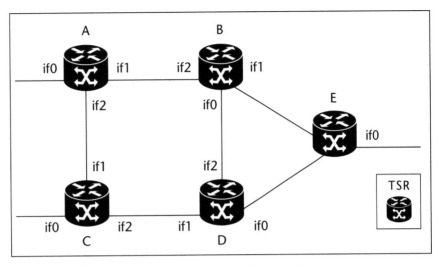

Figure 5.1 *Destination-based forwarding with Tag Switching.*

Table 5.1 shows the state of the TFIB entries associated with 192.6/16. Note that each line represents an entry from the TFIB of a different TSR.

Observe that at this point none of the entries have their outgoing tags populated. This is because so far we only covered local bindings, and local binding doesn't provide the information about the outgoing tags.

Table 5.1   Initial TFIB entries.

	Incoming tag	Outgoing tag	Next hop	Outgoing interface
On TSR A	100	?	TSR B	if1
On TSR B	6	?	TSR E	if1
On TSR C	17	?	TSR D	if2
On TSR D	5	?	TSR E	if0
On TSR E	6	?	TSR E	if0

Now consider what happens once each of these TSRs starts to distribute information about its local binding to other TSRs and how this information is used to populate the outgoing tags. TSR A sends the information about its local binding to B and C. However, when B receives this information, it notices that it didn't come from B's next hop for 192.6/16. So, TSR B can't use this information for the purpose of updating the outgoing tag of the TFIB entry associated with 192.6/16. The same applies when C receives this information.

TSR B sends the information about its local binding to A, D, and E. Because neither D nor E uses B as its next hop for 192.6/16, neither of these TSRs can use this information for the purpose of updating the outgoing tag in their TFIB entries for 192.6/16. However, when TSR A receives this information, it notices that this information came from its next hop for 192.6/16. Therefore, TSR A uses this information as a remote binding for 192.6/16 and uses the tag provided by this information (tag 6) to update the outgoing tag in its TFIB entry associated with 192.6/16. At this point A has a fully populated entry in its TFIB.

The local binding information that TSR C sends to A and D is not going to be used by either of them, since neither of them use C as the next hop for 192.6/16.

The local binding information that D sends to B, C, and E is used only by C, since only C uses D as its next hop for 192.6/16. Once TSR C receives this information, it populates the outgoing tag of the TFIB entry associated with 192.6/16 with the tag received as part of this information (tag 5).

The local binding information that TSR E sends to B and D is used by both of these TSRs, as both B and D use E as the next hop for 192.6/16. So, as soon as B and D receive this information, they update the outgoing tag in their TFIB entry associated with 192.6/16 with the tag carried as part of this information.

The TFIB entries associated with 192.6/16 at this point are given in Table 5.2.

Table 5.2 TFIB entries after tag distribution.

	Incoming tag	Outgoing tag	Next hop	Outgoing interface
On TSR A	100	6	TSR E	if1
On TSR B	6	6	TSR E	if1
On TSR C	17	5	TSR D	if2
On TSR D	5	6	TSR E	if0
On TSR E	6	?	TSR E	if0

Note that on TSR E there is still no outgoing tag in the TFIB entry for 192.6/16. Moreover, the next hop in this entry points to itself (TSR E). This is because 192.6/16 is directly connected to E. When E receives a packet that carries tag 6, TSR E acts as an edge TSR and just strips the tag from the packet.

At this point all the TSRs have their entries for 192.6/16 fully populated. Now let's look at the actual packet forwarding. When TSR A receives a packet, and the packet carries tag 100, A uses this tag as an index in its TFIB to locate the entry that A will use for forwarding. Once the entry is found (the incoming tag in the entry is equal to the tag carried in the packet), A replaces (swaps) the tag carried in the packet (tag 100) with the outgoing tag from the found entry (tag 6) and sends it to TSR B over its outgoing interface if1. When TSR B receives this packet, it uses the tag carried in the packet (tag 6) as an index to locate the entry that it will use for forwarding. Once the entry is found (the incoming tag in the entry is equal to the tag carried in the packet), TSR B replaces (swaps) the tag carried in the packet (tag 6) with the outgoing tag from the found entry (tag 6), and sends it to E over its outgoing interface if1. When E receives this packet, it just strips the tag from the packet and delivers it to its destination (which is reachable via if0 on TSR E).

Behavior During Routing Changes

To illustrate how Tag Switching works in the presence of changes in the network topology, let's look at what happens when the link between TSRs D and E goes down. Once D detects that the link is down, it uses the information provided by the unicast routing protocol(s) to change its next hop for 192.6/16 from TSR E to TSR B. As a result, the outgoing tag in TSR D's TFIB entry associated with 192.6/16 is no longer valid. To provide a correct outgoing tag for that entry, D needs to get tag binding information from its new next hop, TSR B. Obtaining this information depends on how B treats tag binding information received from TSRs that are not next hops for the FECs carried as part of this information. If D keeps the tag binding information it received from B, then as soon as D determines its new next hop (TSR B), it can immediately use this information to populate the outgoing tag. Otherwise, if D doesn't keep this information, it would need to rerequest this information from its new next hop, TSR B.

Observe that creation of tag binding is driven by creation of a mapping between a particular FEC and its next hop, which, in turn, is driven by routing updates. Therefore, according to the taxonomy presented in Chapter 2, Tag Switching uses control-driven creation of tag binding. Also observe that whereas the binding between an incoming tag and an FEC is created locally by a TSR (local binding), the binding between an outgoing tag and the FEC is created as a result of receiving the tag binding information (remote binding) from the next hop TSR associated with that FEC. Thus tag switching uses downstream label binding in our taxonomy. Finally, note that the only prerequisite for a TSR to create its local binding for a particular FEC is the availability of the mapping between this FEC and its next hop; specifically the TSR doesn't have to wait for the matching remote binding before creating its local binding. In terms of the taxonomy, tag switching uses independent creation of label switching forwarding table entries.

5.1.2 *Improving Routing Scalability via a Hierarchy of Routing Knowledge*

Recall that one of the design goals of Tag Switching is to improve scaling properties of the routing system. Tag Switching addresses this goal via the notion of a hierarchy of routing knowledge. To help us understand what hierarchy of routing knowledge means, we briefly review some aspects of the Internet routing architecture.

The routing architecture used today in the Internet models the Internet as a collection of routing domains, where routing within individual domains is provided by intradomain routing protocols (e.g., OSPF, RIP, EIGRP), whereas routing across multiple domains is provided by interdomain routing protocols (e.g., BGP). One of the advantages of partitioning routing into intra- and interdomain components is the reduction in the volume of routing information that has to be maintained by routers, which is essential to providing scalable routing. However, this partitioning at the level of routing protocols doesn't result in a complete partition of routing information. Specifically, every router within a transit routing domain (a domain that carries traffic that neither originates in the domain nor is destined to a node in the domain) has to maintain in its forwarding tables all the routes provided by the interdomain routing, regardless of whether this is an interior router (a router connected only to the routers within the same routing domain as the router itself) or a border router (a router connected both to routers within the same routing domain and to routers in other routing domains). Maintaining all the routes provided by the interdomain routing at all the routers, including all the interior routers, is necessary in order to forward the transit traffic through the domain.

Note that the interior routers in a transit domain are basically just transferring packets from one border router to another, so it seems somewhat wasteful for them to have to maintain complete routing tables for all routes in the Internet. Tag Switching provides a means by which those routers can store only the routing information they really need—just enough to get packets to the right border router, where full routing information is still maintained.

Specifically, the interior routers within a domain would have to maintain routes only to the destinations within the domain, rather than to all the destinations in the Internet.

We can think of this as a further step in the hierarchical partitioning of intra- and interdomain routing. This partitioning would reduce the routing load on the interior routers, which in turn would result in better (faster) convergence. It would also provide better fault isolation, as interior routers would be totally immune to any problems in the interdomain routing. Faster convergence, and better fault isolation, would result in improved scalability of the routing system.

Construction of TFIBs to support a hierarchy of routing knowledge is based on the procedures used to support the destination-based forwarding with Tag Switching. All the TSRs within a routing domain participate in a common intradomain routing protocol and employ procedures described in Section 5.1.1 to construct entries in their TFIBs for the FECs associated with the destinations within the domain. These entries are sufficient to provide Tag Switching from any TSR within the domain to any destination within the domain, including all the border TSRs of that domain. Because an ingress border router can determine the egress border router to which it wants to send a packet, a packet can be Tag Switched all the way to the egress of the domain by interior TSRs that know only interior routes.

To enable the border TSRs to perform Tag Switching as well, all the border TSRs within a domain and the directly connected border TSRs in different domains may also create and exchange tag binding information for every route (and FEC associated with that route) received via interdomain routing (BGP). Again, the creation and exchange of this tag binding information follows the procedures described in Section 5.1.1, except that the notion of the "next hop" TSR is generalized to include the next border TSR. Specifically, when a border TSR, TSR A, receives tag binding information from another border TSR, TSR B, and TSR A has the local binding for the FEC carried as part of the tag binding information received from TSR B, TSR A checks whether B is the next border TSR for the FEC (the information needed to perform this check is provided by BGP). If that is the case, then TSR A locates an entry in its TFIB that contains the binding for that FEC and updates the outgoing tag of that entry with the tag carried as part of the received binding information.

As a result of the procedures described above, the TFIB of a border TSR contains entries for FECs corresponding to both inter- and intradomain routes, whereas the TFIB of an interior TSR contains entries for FECs corresponding to only the intradomain routes.

To support forwarding in the presence of a hierarchy of routing knowledge, Tag Switching allows a packet to carry not one, but several tags organized as a tag stack. When a packet is forwarded from one routing domain to another, the tag stack carried by the packet contains just one tag. However, when a packet is forwarded through a transit routing domain, the tag stack contains not one, but two tags. For the purpose of finding a TFIB entry that should be used for forwarding, a TSR always uses the tag at the top of the stack. When a packet carries a stack of tags, a TSR, in addition to swapping the tag at the top of the stack, could also push or pop a tag onto/off of the stack. Pushing tags onto and popping tags off of the stack occur at the domain boundaries. At the ingress a tag is pushed onto the tag stack, and at the egress a tag is popped off of the stack.

To illustrate how Tag Switching supports a hierarchy of routing knowledge, consider the example shown in Figure 5.2. Routing domain A consists of two border TSRs, TSR T and TSR W, and two interior TSRs, TSR X and TSR Y. There is a set of destinations (an address prefix) in routing domain C that is reachable through the border TSR of that domain (TSR Z). TSR Z distributes the routing information about these destinations to TSR W, which in turn distributes it to TSR T, which in turn distributes it to TSR V.

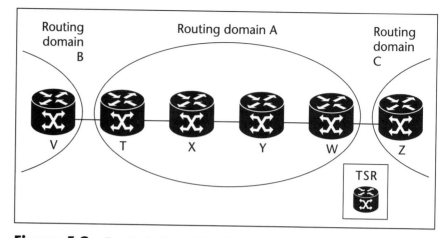

Figure 5.2   *Tag Switching with a hierarchy of routing knowledge.*

Because all the TSRs within A participate in A's intradomain routing, they all have routes to each other. That means that TSR T, TSR X, and TSR Y all have a route to TSR W. Each of these TSRs creates a local binding for that route and distributes information about this binding to other TSRs. Using a combination of local and remote bindings TSR T, TSR X, and TSR Y construct a TFIB entry associated with TSR W, as shown in Table 5.3.

Note that the next hop in the TSR W's TFIB entry points to itself (TSR W). This is used to indicate to TSR W that when it receives a packet with the tag that matches this entry (tag 17), it has to pop off the top tag of the stack carried by the packet. TSR W then performs another lookup in its TFIB using the tag at the top of the stack (after the stack has been popped) and uses the entry determined by this lookup for the actual packet forwarding.

Table 5.3   **TFIB entries in routing domain A.**

	Incoming tag	Outgoing tag	Next hop
On TSR T	N/A	10	TSR X
On TSR X	10	12	TSR Y
On TSR Y	12	17	TSR W
On TSR W	17	N/A	TSR W

So far we have described how TSRs within routing domain A populate their TFIBs with entries associated with the intradomain routes (and more specifically with routes to TSR W). Now let's look at how border TSRs (TSR T, TSR W, TSR V, and TSR Z) populate their TFIBs with entries associated with interdomain routes.

Assume that TSR Z creates a local binding for the FEC associated with the set of destinations in C, with 6 as the local tag. Following the procedures described in Section 5.1.1, TSR Z distributes this binding information to TSR W. Further, assume that TSR W creates a local binding for the same FEC with 2 as the local tag. Following the procedures described in Section 5.1.1, TSR W distributes this binding information to TSR T. When TSR W receives tag binding information from its next hop border TSR (TSR Z), TSR W uses the tag carried in this binding (6) as the outgoing tag. Finally assume that TSR T creates a local binding between the FEC with 5 as the local tag. Following the procedures described in Section 5.1.1, TSR T distributes this binding information to TSR V. When TSR T receives tag binding information from its next hop border TSR (TSR W), TSR T uses the tag carried in this binding (2) as the outgoing tag.

When TSR T receives a tag binding from its next hop border router TSR W, TSR T notices that the next hop associated with the binding (TSR W) is not directly connected to TSR T. Therefore, TSR T looks in its TFIB for the entry that corresponds to the address of the next hop (TSR W). The outgoing tag from the found entry (tag 10) is the tag that TSR T has to push onto the tag stack of a packet whose tag is 5.

Now let's consider packet forwarding and assume that TSR T receives from TSR V a packet with tag 5. TSR T finds that the outgoing tag in its TFIB entry with incoming tag 5 is 2. So, TSR T replaces (swaps) the tag carried in the packet with tag 2. In addition, TSR T pushes tag 10 onto the tag stack carried by the packet, and then sends the packet to the next hop (TSR X). When TSR X receives the packet, it finds in its TFIB an entry with incoming tag 10. The outgoing tag in the found entry is 12, and the next hop is TSR Y. So, TSR X replaces the tag carried in the packet with 12 and sends the packet to the next hop (TSR Y). When TSR Y receives the packet, it replaces the tag carried in the packet with 17 and sends it to TSR W. Finally, when TSR W receives the packet, it finds that the entry in its TFIB whose incoming tag is 17 indicates that the TSR has to pop the label stack. After TSR W pops the stack, the tag at the top of the stack (label 2) will be the tag that was placed there by TSR T. TSR W uses this tag as an index in its TFIB to find an entry whose incoming tag is equal to the tag in the packet. Using the information from the found entry, TSR W replaces the tag carried in the packet with tag 6 and sends the packet to TSR Z.

To summarize, the use of a hierarchy of routing knowledge allows complete isolation of the interior routers within a routing domain from interdomain routing, thus improving the stability and scalability of routing.

5.1.3 *Multicast*

Fundamental to multicast routing is the notion of a *multicast distribution tree*. Such a tree is constructed by multicast routing protocols (e.g., DVMRP, PIM, CBT, MOSPF) and is used by the forwarding component of network layer routing to forward multicast packets. In this section we describe how Tag Switching supports multicast, when the multicast distribution trees are constructed by PIM.

To support multicast with Tag Switching, a TSR should be able to select a particular multicast distribution tree based solely on (a) the tag carried in a packet and (b) the interface on which the packet was received. As we mentioned in Chapter 2, this requires a TSR to maintain its TFIB on a per-interface basis and also imposes the following two requirements on the Tag Switching control component:

- No two TSRs connected to a common subnetwork may bind the same tag on that subnetwork to different multicast distribution trees.

- TSRs that are connected to a common subnetwork, and are part of a common multicast distribution tree, have to agree among themselves on a common tag that will be used by all these TSRs when sending and receiving packets associated with that tree on the interfaces connected to that subnetwork.

Let's look at how Tag Switching addresses these two requirements.

Note that the first requirement is always satisfied when TSRs are connected on a point-to-point subnetwork. To satisfy the first requirement when TSRs are connected on a multiaccess subnetwork (e.g., Ethernet), Tag Switching defines procedures by which such TSRs partition the set of tags that they use for multicast into disjoint subsets, with each TSR getting its own subset. Each TSR advertises via PIM HELLO messages a range of tags that the TSR wants to use for its local bindings. When a TSR connected to a multiaccess subnetwork boots up, it checks that the range it wants to use is disjoint from the ranges used by other TSRs connected to the same subnetwork by listening to the PIM HELLO message received on its interface connected to the subnetwork. If a TSR receives from some other TSR a PIM HELLO message with a range of tags that overlaps with the range of tags it is advertising in its PIM HELLO messages, one of these TSRs has to get another range of tags. Maintaining TFIBs for multicast on a per-interface (rather than on a per-TSR) basis allows a TSR to perform the above procedures on a per-interface basis. The range of tags that the TSR gets (and uses) on one of its interfaces is completely independent from the range of tags the TSR gets on another interface(s).

To meet the second requirement Tag Switching defines procedures by which TSRs that are connected to a common subnetwork and are part of a common multicast distribution tree elect among themselves one particular TSR that will be responsible for creating a local binding for the FEC associated with that tree and defines procedures for distributing this binding information among these TSRs.

To join a particular multicast distribution tree, a TSR, just like a conventional router, needs to send a PIM JOIN message toward the root of that tree. To create a local binding for that tree, the TSR takes a tag from the pool of tags associated with the interface over which the message should be sent and creates an entry in its TFIB with the incoming tag set to the tag taken from the pool of tags. The TSR then includes this tag in the PIM JOIN message and sends the message toward the root of the tree. When a TSR that is a part of a particular multicast distribution tree receives a PIM JOIN message from a downstream (with respect to the root of the tree) TSR, the TSR updates the entry in its TFIB that corresponds to the tree with the tag carried by the message and the interface on which the message was received. Specifically, the TSR uses the tag to populate the outgoing tag in the entry, and the interface to populate the outgoing interface in the entry.

The procedure we described in the previous paragraph is sufficient to meet the second requirement when TSRs are connected on a point-to-point subnetwork. Now let's look at how this works when TSRs are connected on a multiaccess subnetwork. Observe that on multiaccess subnetworks PIM JOIN messages are multicasted. Thus all the TSRs connected to a multiaccess subnetwork receive all the PIM JOIN messages transmitted by any of these TSRs over the interfaces connected to the subnetwork. The first TSR on that subnetwork that decides to join a particular multicast distribution tree is the TSR that creates the binding between a tag and the tree. All other TSRs on the subnetwork receive information about this binding from the PIM JOIN message that the TSR sends toward the root of the tree, as the TSR periodically sends this message, and this message is multicasted to all the TSRs connected to the subnetwork. Thus any TSR connected to the subnetwork that decides later on to join the multicast distribution tree would know the tag that is bound to the tree on that subnetwork. As that TSR joins the tree, it uses the tag from the received PIM JOIN message as an incoming tag for its TFIB entry associated with the tree. If a TSR connected to a particular subnetwork wants to determine whether a binding for a particular multicast tree among other TSRs connected to that subnetwork already exists, the TSR sends the PIM JOIN message with 0 as the tag. When some other TSR (connected to the same subnetwork) receives this message, and that other TSR already has the binding, that other TSR sends a PIM JOIN message that includes the tag associated with the binding. Because TSRs maintain their TFIBs used for multicast on a per-interface (rather than on a per-TSR) basis, a TSR can apply the procedure described above on a per-interface basis, without requiring coordination among the procedures the TSR applies on each of its interfaces.

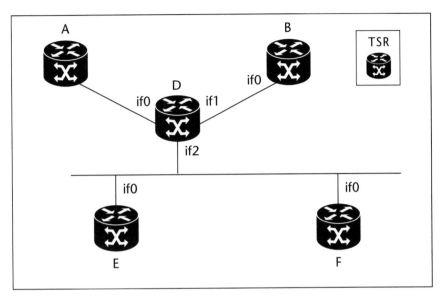

Figure 5.3   *Multicast with Tag Switching.*

To illustrate how Tag Switching supports multicast, consider an example shown in Figure 5.3, where TSR D, TSR E, and TSR F are connected on a multiaccess subnetwork (e.g., Ethernet), while all other connections are on point-to-point subnetworks.

Let's assume that there is a multicast tree rooted at TSR A and that this tree initially includes just TSR A and TSR D. When TSR B wants to join the tree, it has to send a PIM JOIN message toward TSR A, which means that B has to send this message on its interface if0. Before sending this message, B takes a tag from the pool of free tags associated with its interface if0 and creates in its TFIB an entry with this tag as an incoming tag. TSR B then sends the PIM JOIN message that includes this tag to TSR D. When D receives this message, it finds in its TFIB an entry that corresponds to the tree, and then it adds the tag that was received in the message as an outgoing tag for the entry and adds the interface on which the message was received (interface if1) as an outgoing interface. This covers the case where connection from a TSR toward the root of a multicast distribution tree is via a point-to-point subnetwork.

Next we'll look at the case where the connection is via a multi-access subnetwork.

Consider what would happen when TSR E decides to join the tree. To join the tree E has to send a PIM JOIN message toward TSR A, which means that E has to send this message on its interface if0 to D. Before sending this message, E takes a tag from the pool of free tags associated with the interface on which the message has to be sent (interface if0) and creates in its TFIB an entry with this tag as an incoming tag. TSR E then sends a PIM JOIN message that includes this tag. Note that because this message is multicasted, it will be received by all the TSRs connected to the subnetwork, which means that it will be received by TSRs D, E, and F. When TSR D receives this message, it finds in its TFIB an entry that corresponds to the tree, and then it adds the tag that was received in the message as an outgoing tag for the entry and adds the interface on which the message was received (interface if2) as an outgoing interface. Note that at this point the entry in D has two outgoing interfaces (if1 and if2) and, corresponding to them, two outgoing tags.

Now assume that TSR F wants to join the same multicast distribution tree. Note that at the time F decides to join the tree, it should already have the tag that is bound to the tree, as this tag was carried in the PIM JOIN messages that were sent (multicasted) by TSR D. So, at this point F finds an entry in its TFIB that corresponds to the tag and sets the incoming tag in the entry to that tag.

For dense-mode multicast groups PIM doesn't require routers to send JOIN messages. To support dense-mode multicast groups with Tag Switching, the PIM dense-mode procedures are modified to require that a TSR send PIM JOIN messages for dense-mode groups as soon as the TSR creates a multicast route for such a group. This modification allows use of a common mechanism for distributing tag binding information that works both for sparse and for dense groups.

One could argue that supporting multicast with Tag Switching by piggybacking tag binding information on top of PIM prevents the use of Tag Switching in the environments where multicast routing is provided by other protocols (e.g., MOSPF, DVMRP).

Although it is certainly true that in the area of multicast the primary focus of Tag Switching was Tag Switching with PIM, Tag Switching also provides a way to distribute tag binding information associated with multicast routes via the Tag Distribution Protocol (TDP). This way, Tag Switching can support multicast with multicast routing protocols other than PIM.

Observe that the creation of tag binding is driven by PIM messages. Therefore, according to the taxonomy presented in Chapter 2, Tag Switching uses control-driven creation of tag binding for multicast. The binding between an outgoing tag and a particular multicast distribution tree is created as a result of receiving tag binding information from a downstream TSR; that is, the downstream mode of binding distribution is used. Note that in order to create a local binding a TSR doesn't need to wait until it receives the matching remote binding. Thus, tag switching uses independent creation of label switching forwarding entries for multicast. Finally, observe that to distribute multicast tag binding information Tag Switching piggybacks this information on top of PIM and does not require a separate protocol for distributing this information.

5.1.4 *RSVP with Tag Switching*

Tag Switching provides support for RSVP by defining a new RSVP Object—the Tag Object. The Tag Object contains tag binding information for an RSVP flow and is carried in the RSVP RESV message.

Supporting RSVP with Tag Switching doesn't impact handling of RSVP PATH messages; these messages are handled in precisely the same way as they are without Tag Switching. The place where Tag Switching imposes additional procedures is the handling of RSVP RESV messages.

In the case of supporting RSVP unicast flows with Tag Switching, when a TSR wants to send a RESV message for a new RSVP flow, the TSR allocates a tag from its pool of free tags, creates an entry in its TFIB with the incoming tag set to the allocated tag, places the tag in the Tag Object, and then sends out the RESV message with this object. The newly created TFIB entry, in addition to tag information, contains information about local resources (e.g., queues) that packets whose tag matches the incoming tag of the entry will use. The information about the local resources to be used is derived from the resource reservation information carried in RSVP. The TSR populates the outgoing tag component as it receives the RESV message from its next hop TSR. Once an RSVP flow is established, the reservation state needs to be refreshed. In this case, a TSR sends RESV messages associated with the flow and includes in them the same tag that the TSR bound to the flow when it first created the RSVP state for the flow.

Observe that the creation of tag binding is driven by RSVP messages; binding is thus control-driven. Because the binding between an outgoing tag and a particular RSVP flow is created as a result of receiving tag binding information (remote binding) from a downstream TSR, the label distribution is once again downstream. Observe that in order to create a local binding, a TSR doesn't need to wait until it receives the matching remote binding. Therefore, according to the taxonomy presented in Chapter 2, Tag Switching uses independent creation of label switching forwarding entries for RSVP. Finally, we note that Tag Switching piggybacks the label binding information on top of RSVP and does not require a separate protocol for distributing this information.

5.1.5 *Explicit Routes*

The ability to support forwarding paradigms other than destination-based forwarding is one of the important design goals of Tag Switching. In this section we outline how Tag Switching can support *explicit* routes, by which we mean routes that are explicitly chosen to be other than the normal route chosen by the routing protocols. Such a route may, for example, be chosen to manage the load on a particular link (see Section 1.1.4 in Chapter 1 for an example).

Tag Switching provides support for explicit routes by using the Resource Reservation Protocol (RSVP), and defining a new RSVP Object—the Explicit Route Object. The Explicit Route Object is used to specify a particular explicit route. This object is carried in the RSVP PATH message. The tag binding information for the route is carried in the Tag Object by the RSVP RESV message, as described in the previous section.

The Explicit Route Object itself is composed of a sequence of variable-length subobjects, where each subobject identifies a single hop within an explicit route. Each subobject contains a strict/loose indicator, followed by the type, length, and value. The Type field allows individual hops to be expressed as either an IPv4 address prefix, an IPv6 address prefix, or an Autonomous System number. Expressing individual hops as IPv4 (or IPv6) addresses is accomplished by specifying the appropriate prefix length (32 for IPv4 addresses, 128 for IPv6 addresses). When an individual hop is expressed as an IP (either IPv4 or IPv6) address prefix, this hop includes any TSR that has an IP address that matches the prefix. When an individual hop is expressed as an autonomous system number, this hop includes any TSR that belongs to the autonomous system identified by that autonomous system number.

The ability to express individual hops not just in terms of individual TSRs within a network topology, but in terms of a group of TSRs, provides the routing system with a significant amount of flexibility, as a TSR that computes (establishes) an explicit route need not have detailed information about the route (e.g., all the TSRs along the route). For example, a TSR can establish an explicit route expressed in terms of autonomous systems (by using autonomous system numbers as subobjects), without knowing detailed network topology within each of these autonomous systems.

The Explicit Route Object allows TSRs in the middle of an explicit route carried in the object to modify the explicit route by inserting a sequence of one or more subobjects in the Explicit Route Object. This features adds to the flexibility that is provided by explicit routes by allowing TSRs in the middle of an explicit route to compensate for the lack of the detailed information at the TSR that originated the explicit route.

One of the main motivations for using RSVP to support explicit routes is the assumption that quite often explicit routes will be used in conjunction with reserving resources along such routes. This assumption is based on the expected use of explicit routes in such applications as providing forwarding in support of QoS-based routing. In such cases use of RSVP for supporting explicit routes allows both the establishment of an explicit route and the allocation of resources for the traffic that will be forwarded along the route. This is accomplished just using RSVP, rather than having one protocol for establishing explicit routes and another for making resource reservations along such routes. Note that the use of RSVP for supporting explicit routes doesn't mean that these routes always have to have reserved resources. To the contrary, this mechanism could be used as well to support explicit routes for best effort traffic (traffic that doesn't require any resource reservations).

Use of RSVP for supporting explicit routes with Tag Switching means that RSVP is originated by a router, rather than a host. There is nothing in RSVP that precludes this.

The set of packets that could be forwarded along a particular explicit route is determined solely by the TSR that establishes the route. In other words, the rules for determining the set of packets that would map into a Forwarding Equivalence Class associated with that explicit route are purely local to the TSR that establishes the route. For example, these rules may include such criteria as the interface on the TSR that the packets arrive on, or time of day. Explicit routes provide such flexibility because rules for determining mapping between packets and FECs are purely local to a TSR that establishes an explicit route and require no coordination among TSRs. Different TSRs could establish explicit routes without any coordination of the rules each of them uses for determining the mapping. Because the rules by which a TSR that establishes an explicit route maps packets into FECs are purely local to the TSR, there is no need to standardize them.

The creation of label bindings in support of explicit routes with RSVP is much the same as in the pure RSVP case. Similarly, all of the observations about how Tag Switching with RSVP fits into the taxonomy described in Chapter 2 apply in the case of explicit routes as well.

5.2 Tag Switching over ATM

In this section we describe how Tag Switching operates on ATM switches. We refer to such switches as ATM-TSRs. Because ATM and Tag Switching use precisely the same forwarding paradigm, label swapping, Tag Switching can use ATM forwarding ("ATM User Plane") pretty much "as is." This means that Tag Switching can run on unmodified ATM switch hardware. Although it preserves the ATM User Plane, Tag Switching replaces the ATM Control Plane with the Tag Switching Control Component. Supporting Tag Switching on a ATM switch means that operations of the switch are controlled by the Tag Switching control component rather than by the protocols defined by either the ITU or ATM Forum. Thus an ATM-TSR controls its operations by running protocols such as OSPF, BGP, PIM, and RSVP, rather than protocols such as UNI and PNNI.

When Tag Switching is used with ATM switches, the forwarding performance of such a device is determined by the capabilities of the ATM switches, whereas its functionality is comparable to a router. This is because, from the forwarding point of view, it is totally irrelevant whether the ATM forwarding table is constructed using the Tag Switching control component or using UNI, PNNI, and so forth. And from the functionality point of view, the functionality is determined largely by the control component, rather than by specifics of how such a device forwards data.

We begin the discussion by describing how tag information can be carried when Tag Switching operates over ATM switches. Then we describe modifications to the procedures used by non–ATM TSRs in order to support Tag Switching on ATM TSRs.

5.2.1 Carrying Tag Information

When Tag Switches are built out of ATM-TSRs, tag information is carried in the ATM header. If the tag stack has just one level of tags, then the tag is carried in the VCI field of the header. Because the size of the VCI field is 16 bits, that allows up to 2^{16} tags. Because the forwarding tables of ATM switches are usually organized on a per-interface basis, when tags are carried in the VCI field the total number of tags on an ATM-TSR can be more than 2^{16}. If the tag stack has two levels of tags (as described in Section 5.1.2), then the first level is carried in the VCI field, and the second level can be carried in the VPI field of the header. Note that because the size of the VPI field is 12 bits, a limit is imposed of 4096 tags (2^{12}) that can be carried in the VPI field per interface.

A predefined VCI/VPI is reserved for exchanging tag binding information. Use of a predefined VCI/VPI is necessary to bootstrap the system.

5.2.2 *Destination-Based Forwarding*

Supporting destination-based forwarding on an ATM-TSR involves some modifications to the procedures Tag Switching uses to support destination-based forwarding on a non–ATM TSR. In this section we highlight these modifications.

The most important modification is that remote binding is always acquired *on-demand*. Acquiring remote binding on-demand means two things. First, an ATM-TSR doesn't advertise its local binding to another TSR until that other TSR sends a request for this binding. Second, in order to receive information about the remote binding from some other TSR, the TSR has to explicitly send a request to that other TSR. Acquiring remote binding on-demand allows conservation of the use of tags, which may be important because ATM switches normally have some hardware limitations on the number of tags they can support. On-demand binding also deals with the problem of cell interleave, which we will now examine.

To understand the problem of cell interleave, consider an example shown in Figure 5.4a, and assume that the TFIB associated with both if0 and if1 on ATM TSR X contains the following entry:

Incoming tag	Outgoing tag	Outgoing interface
7	3	if2

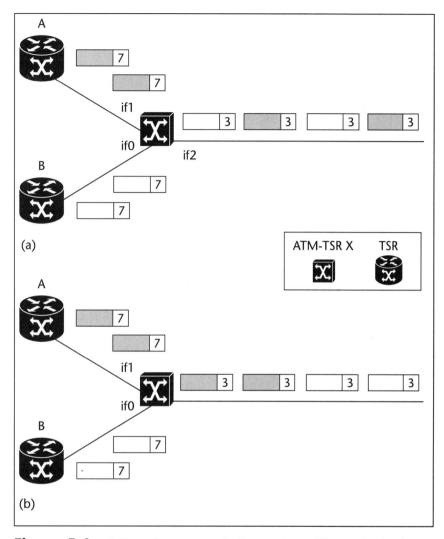

Figure 5.4 *Cell interleave example. Frames from different destinations are interleaved by conventional switch (a); VC-merge delays cells of one frame to prevent interleaving with another (b).*

Now consider what would happen when both TSR A and TSR B each send a packet with tag 7. First these packets are broken into ATM cells by the ATM interfaces on TSR A and TSR B. Then each of these TSRs transmits these cells to ATM-TSR X. Let's assume that the first cell that is received by ATM-TSR X is the cell that was sent by B. X performs normal ATM forwarding procedures, replaces VCI 7 with VCI 3, and sends the cell on interface if2 to the next hop. Assume that the next cell that is received by X is the cell that was sent by TSR A. As it did with the previous cell, X replaces VCI 7 with VCI 3 and sends the cell on interface if2 to the next hop. Now assume that the next cell received by ATM-TSR X is again the cell that was sent by TSR A. X replaces VCI 7 with VCI 3 and sends the cell to the next hop.

Observe that cells that ATM-TSR X sends on its interface if2 form an intermix in the sense that two consecutive cells sent on this interface may belong to different packets. As a result, the next hop (not shown in the figure) wouldn't be able to correctly reassemble these cells into packets. This is the problem of cell interleave: the procedures described above result in a cell stream in which cells from different packets are interleaved.

One way to eliminate cell interleave is to require an ATM-TSR not to interspread cells from different packets when forwarding these cells. That, in turn, requires the ATM-TSR to buffer cells that are part of a single packet until the last cell of that packet is received. Once the last cell is received, the ATM-TSR sends all the cells that are part of the packet. Moreover, the ATM-TSR sends all these cells without interspreading them with cells from other packets. This approach is known as *VC-merge*.

Using the example shown in Figure 5.4b, when ATM-TSR X receives a cell with VCI 7 on its interface if0, X checks whether this cell carried the end-of-packet indicator and, if not, places the cell into a buffer associated with the interface if0. Likewise, when X receives a cell with VCI 7 on its interface if1, X checks whether the cell carries the end-of-packet indicator and, if not, places the cell into a buffer associated with the interface if1. As soon as X receives a cell with VCI 7 on an interface if0, and the cell carries the end-of-packet indicator, X sends out all the cells stored in the buffer associated with if0 and then transmits the cell with the end-of-packet indicator as well. X sends these cells without interspreading them with other cells on the same VC.

Using the VC-merge approach requires an ATM-TSR to be able to detect cells with the end-of-packet indicator and to buffer cells based on the packet boundaries. Although neither of these requirements is part of the ATM standards, from a practical point of view both of these requirements are either already supported or likely to be supported by ATM switches. In fact, the first requirement (the ability to detect cells with the end-of-packet indicator) is necessary to perform such algorithms as Early Packet Discard (EPD) and Partial Packet Discard (PPD), and both of these algorithms are necessary to improve handling of frame-based traffic in the presence of congestion within an ATM network.

Note that VC-merge is used in Tag Switching just to support destination-based routing; it isn't used for traffic that requires resource reservations. Therefore, the impact of buffering (the result of VC-merge) on such factors as jitter is not important.

Another way to eliminate cell interleave is to maintain more than one tag associated with a particular route. To understand how that would help to solve the cell interleave problem, observe that one of the necessary conditions for cell interleave is for ATM cells that belong to different packets to have the same VCI field. If cells from different packets had different VCIs, there would be no confusion when these cells needed to be reassembled into packets. In fact, it isn't even necessary for each packet to have its own VCI—all the packets that are forwarded along the same route by a particular TSR at the edge of a network composed just of ATM-TSRs could use the same VCI. This observation suggests the following procedure for creating and distributing tag binding information in support of destination-based forwarding on ATM-TSRs.

When a TSR at the edge of a network composed just of ATM-TSRs creates a local binding, and the next hop of the route associated with the binding is an ATM-TSR, the TSR sends a message (using the Tag Distribution Protocol) to the ATM-TSR requesting that this ATM-TSR create a binding for the route and return binding information to the TSR. When an ATM-TSR receives the request, the ATM-TSR creates a local binding and returns this binding to the requestor. In addition, the ATM-TSR sends a message (using the Tag Distribution Protocol) to the next hop associated with the route, requesting that this next hop create a binding for the route.

One of the advantages of using multiple tags per route is that it doesn't require any modifications to ATM hardware, and therefore can be used with any ATM switch. With respect to the number of VCs required, this approach scales similarly to the IP over ATM approach described in Section 1.1.3 (which will generally produce a complete mesh of VCs). However, with respect to the amount of routing peering required, this approach scales much better than the IP over ATM approach, as routing peering with Tag Switching is constrained by the physical connectivity. Clearly, with respect to the number of VCs required, this approach scales less well than the approach based on VC-merge.

5.3 Tag Encapsulation on Non-ATM Links

With some link layer technologies (e.g., ATM), the link layer header has adequate semantics to carry tag information. For such technologies, carrying tag information in the link layer header has an advantage of allowing the re-use of existing forwarding functionality (e.g., the ability to use ATM switch hardware). However, there are other link layer technologies (e.g., point-to-point links, Ethernet, FDDI, Token Ring, etc.), whose link layer headers don't have semantics adequate to carry tag information. When Tag Switching is used over subnetworks built out of such technologies, tag information is carried in a small "shim" inserted between the link layer and the network layer headers.

On point-to-point subnetworks, packets that carry tags are identified by the PPP protocol field, with one value used to identify unicast and another to identify multicast. On multiaccess subnetworks such packets are identified by the ethertype. Like point-to-point subnetworks, multiaccess subnetworks use one ethertype to identify unicast and another to identify multicast.

To support the notion of a tag stack as discussed in Section 5.1.2, the shim layer used by Tag Switching consists of a sequence of tag stack entries, where the top of the tag stack appears in a packet right after the link layer header, and the bottom of the tag stack appears in the packet right before the network layer header. Packet forwarding is determined by the entry at the top of the stack. Each tag stack entry is encoded as shown in Figure 5.5.

The S field is used to indicate an entry that is at the bottom of the tag stack—this entry has the S field set to 1. All other entries have this field set to 0.

The Time-to-Live (TTL) field is similar to the Time-to-Live field carried in the IP header. Note that a TSR processes only the TTL field of the top entry.

The Class of Service (CoS) field is intended to influence the queuing decision by TSRs. When an edge TSR tags a previously untagged packet, the value of the CoS field is determined by the policies local to the edge TSR. When a TSR pushes an additional entry onto the tag stack, the TSR sets the value of the CoS field in the newly pushed entry to either the CoS field from the entry that was at the top of the stack prior to the push, or to a value determined by the policies local to the TSR. The CoS field can be used in a way similar to the way the IP Precedence field is used (e.g., to differentiate between different classes of users). Because there is no common agreement on the exact semantics of the IP Precedence field at the time of this writing, it is fairly hard to be specific on the exact semantics of the CoS field as well.

Tag (20 bits)	CoS (3 bits)	S (1 bit)	TTL (8 bits)

Figure 5.5 *Tag stack entry format.*

The tag field contains the value that a TSR uses as an index in its TFIB. Note that the size of this field (20 bits) allows for up to 1,048,576 tags. Because unicast packets are distinguished from multicast packets by either PPP protocol field (on point-to-point subnetworks) or by ethertype (on multiaccess subnetworks), this allows for up to 1,048,576 tags for multicast, and 1,048,576 tags for unicast. In principle, the tag space could be increased by assigning additional PPP protocol fields or ethertypes. In practice, the number of usable tags is more likely to be limited by factors other than the tag space, such as the number of routes that can be supported.

Because inserting the shim layer in a packet increases the length of the packet, and because performing IP fragmentation is undesirable, especially along a Tag Switched path, Tag Switching uses the IP Path MTU Discovery procedures to ensure that even after the shim layer is added to the packet, the resulting packet size doesn't exceed the maximum packet size that could be transmitted without fragmentation.

Use of the shim layer allows TSRs to communicate over LANs that include existing link layer bridges without imposing any additional requirements on such bridges.

5.4 Handling Tag Faults

When a TSR receives a packet with a tag, but either (a) there is no entry in the TFIB maintained by the TSR with the incoming tag equal to the tag carried in the packet or (b) there is such an entry, but the entry doesn't indicate local delivery and the outgoing tag component of the entry is empty, we call this condition a *tag fault*. In this section we describe how Tag Switching handles this problem.

When a TSR encounters a tag fault caused by a packet, one possible option for the TSR is to strip the tag information from the packet and try to forward the packet based on the information carried in the network layer header of the packet. However, this option may not always be feasible. For example, when a packet carries a stack of tags, the TSR may not have sufficient routing information to forward the packet (e.g., TSR X in Figure 5.2 has routing information only about destinations within its own routing domain and thus doesn't know how to forward a packet destined to a host in some other routing domain). When the TSR is an ATM-TSR, requiring the TSR to forward the packet based on the network layer header would require the ATM-TSR to reassemble ATM cells that form the packet into a packet and then process the network layer header of the packet. Clearly, this may be a rather unreasonable requirement.

Because handling tag faults by stripping tag information and forwarding the packet based on the information carried in the network layer header is not always feasible, Tag Switching makes this optional for a TSR. If a TSR can't support this option, then the TSR, when it encounters a tag fault, discards the packet that caused the tag fault. Note that this behavior (discarding a packet) is very similar to the behavior of a conventional router when it receives a packet but doesn't have the routing information needed to forward the packet (which could happen, for example, during routing transients).

5.5 Handling Forwarding Loops During Routing Transients

As we discussed in Section 5.2, because routing protocols used by the Control Component may produce temporary (transient) forwarding loops, we need mechanism(s) to contain the adverse effects of these loops. In this section we describe the mechanisms used by Tag Switching.

For the cases where tag information is carried in a packet in a shim, Tag Switching uses the time-to-live as the loop mitigation mechanism. The shim header contains the TTL field; each TSR that forwards a packet decrements this field; if a TSR receives a packet with TTL in the shim equal to 0, the TSR discards the packet. The effectiveness of this mechanism is comparable to the TTL-based loop mitigation used in IP. Moreover, use of a common mechanism by both IP and Tag Switching makes coexistence and interoperation between loop mitigation mechanisms used by Tag Switching and IP a nonissue.

For the cases where tag information is carried as part of the link layer header (e.g., ATM, Frame Relay), use of time-to-live–based loop mitigation is not a viable option because there is no TTL field in the ATM or Frame Relay header. For these cases, Tag Switching uses a two-pronged approach. First, all the traffic exchanged by the Tag Switching Control Component (e.g., routing traffic, Tag Distribution Protocol) is segregated from the rest of the traffic by using a separate tag (e.g., separate VCI/VPI for the case of ATM) and allocating resources (e.g., buffers, link bandwidth) for that tag. This prevents the detrimental effects of transient forwarding loops on control traffic (which includes routing traffic as well). This, in turn, guarantees that such transient forwarding loops do not affect routing convergence. Furthermore, many ATM-TSRs employ per-VC buffering and queuing. This isolates traffic that follows different routes by constraining the amount of resources that could be consumed by traffic that follows a particular route. As a result, if a route forms a (transient) forwarding loop, the amount of resources that could be consumed by packets forwarded by using this route would be constrained, which, in turn, constrains the negative impact of forwarding loops on traffic that has to be forwarded along nonlooping paths.

The second mechanism to avoid loops when ATM-TSRs are involved uses a hop count in the TDP requests and responses. Because the on-demand binding method forces requests to propagate from the point of a topology change toward the egress of the ATM-TSR cloud, transient loops can be detected and broken (as shown in Figure 5.6). The hop count works like a TTL, but it is carried in the TDP messages. When it reaches zero, the request for label bindings fails, and the spiral path shown here is torn down. When routing stabilizes, a new binding request will be issued and a nonlooping path will be established.

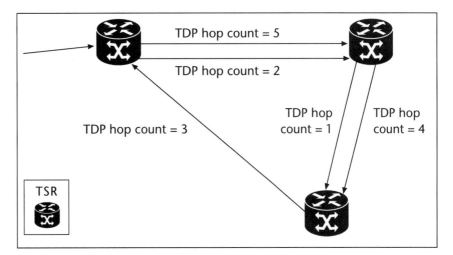

Figure 5.6 *Use of hop count in TDP for loop avoidance.*

5.6 Tag Distribution Protocol (TDP)

For reasons mentioned in Section 2.3.5, Tag Switching views piggybacking tag binding information on top of routing protocols as the preferred way of distributing tag binding information. However, because this option may not always be viable, Tag Switching provides its own mechanism to distribute tag binding information: the Tag Distribution Protocol (TDP). In this section we present a short overview of TDP.

A TSR that exchanges routing information with some other TSR also maintains a TDP session with that other TSR in order to exchange tag binding information for the routes that have been constructed from the exchanged routing information.

Information exchanged via TDP consists of a stream of messages, where each message consists of a fixed header, followed by one or more Protocol Information Elements (PIEs). The fixed header consists of the Version field, followed by the Length field, followed by the TDP identifier field. The Version field identifies a specific version of TDP. The Length field specifies the total length of a message. The TDP Identifier field identifies the TSR that sends the message. Each PIE is encoded as a <Type, Length, Value> structure, where the Type field defines the semantics of the Value field, and the Length field defines the length of the Value field. All the information carried within a PIE is encoded as <Type, Length, Value> as well. Use of the <Type, Length, Value> encoding provides flexibility and extensibility to the protocols.

At the time of this writing TDP defines the following PIEs:

- TDP_PIE_OPEN. This is the first PIE that a TSR sends to another TSR once the TSR opens a TCP connection with the other TSR.

- TDP_PIE_BIND. This PIE is used to convey tag binding information between a pair of TSRs. The binding information consists of a sequence of tag binding entries. For destination-based (unicast) routing, each entry contains a tag and an address prefix. The tag in the entry is the incoming tag associated with the FEC identified by the address prefix on the TSR that sends a TDP_PIE_BIND that contains the entry.

- TDP_PIE_REQUEST_BIND. This PIE allows a TSR to request some other TSR to send the tag binding information to the requestor TSR for a particular FEC (in the case of destination-based routing the FEC is identified by an address prefix) that is maintained by that TSR. The other TSR will use the TDP_PIE_BIND PIE to send this information to the requestor TSR.

- TDP_PIE_WITHDRAW_BIND. This PIE is used by a TSR to withdraw a tag binding that the TSR previously advertised to other TSRs.

- TDP_PIE_RELEASE_BIND. This PIE allows a TSR that received a tag binding as a consequence of sending TDP_PIE_REQUEST_BIND to some other TSR to indicate to that other TSR that the TSR no longer needs the binding. The other TSR, when it receives this PIE, may delete the binding.

- TDP_PIE_KEEP_ALIVE. A TSR uses this PIE to verify "liveness" of another TSR with whom the TSR maintains a TDP session.

- TDP_PIE_NOTIFICATION. This PIE is used to convey any errors.

Exchange of tag binding information via TDP is based on the technique of incremental updates, where only changes to the tag binding information (e.g., creation of a new binding, deletion of an existing binding) are communicated via the protocol. Use of incremental updates requires reliable, in-order delivery of information. To meet this requirement TDP uses TCP as a transport to carry all the TDP messages. This design choice is largely based on the positive experience gained with BGP, where routing information is exchanged via incremental updates and TCP is used as a transport to carry the exchange of the routing information. This approach has very low overhead in the presence of stable topology, because there is no need to refresh any information that has not changed.

5.7 Summary

Tag Switching is an approach to label switching that seeks to address many of the problems described in Chapter 1. These include enhancing routing functionality and improving the scalability and stability of routing. In this respect it has a broader set of goals than the other approaches described so far. It also addresses IP/ATM integration and performance issues.

Tag Switching takes advantage of the flexibility provided by the label switching forwarding component by supporting in its Control Component a wide spectrum of forwarding granularities. At one end of the spectrum, Tag Switching allows FECs to be identified with address prefixes or even whole groups of prefixes, which is essential for providing scalable routing. Tag Switching also allows FECs to be associated with a source/destination address pair. This is essential for supporting multicast with Tag Switching. By associating FECs with a combination of source address, destination address, transport protocol, source port, and destination port, Tag Switching provides support for RSVP and application flows. Finally, Tag Switching allows association with FECs based on purely local rules in order to support explicit routes according to local policy.

Tag Switching allows any number of different FECs to coexist in a single TSR, as long as these FECs provide unambiguous (with respect to that TSR) partitioning of the universe of packets that could be seen by the TSR.

One of the key innovations of Tag Switching is the use of a hierarchy of tags, organized as a tag stack. This enables enhancements to routing scalability by allowing FECs to form a hierarchy that reflects the hierarchy in the underlying routing system.

Notably, Tag Switching has paid more attention to non-ATM links than any other approach. This is reflected both in the encapsulation for frame-based links and in the attention to issues such as tag partitioning on multiaccess media.

In Tag Switching the creation of tag binding information is driven mostly by control, rather than data traffic. Tag Switching uses downstream tag binding. Distribution of tag binding information, whenever practical, is accomplished by piggybacking this information on top of routing protocols. To cover the cases where piggybacking is impractical, Tag Switching provides a separate protocol, TDP, for distributing tag binding information.

Further Reading

There are two published papers on Tag Switching:

Rekhter, Y., B. Davie, D. Katz, E. Rosen, and G. Swallow. *Cisco Systems' Tag Switching Architecture Overview.* RFC 2105, February 1997.

Rekhter, Y., B. Davie, E. Rosen, G. Swallow, D. Farinacci, and D. Katz. "Tag Switching Architecture Overview." In Proceedings of the IEEE 82, no. 12, December 1997, 1973–1983.

There are also many Internet drafts at the usual sites, including

ftp://ds.internic.net/internet-drafts

It is also possible to find a great deal of Tag Switching information at Cisco's Website at

www.cisco.com

For an overview of PIM, we recommend

Deering, S., D. Estrin, D. Farinacci, V. Jacobson, C. Gung Liu, and L. Wei. "An Architecture for Wide-area Multicast Routing." In Proceedings of ACM SIGCOMM 94, London, September 1994.

Chapter

6

Aggregate Route-Based IP Switching (ARIS)

The ARIS proposal has much in common with Tag Switching, especially when one considers the core of each proposal: the handling of destination-based routing. They are much closer to each other than they are to any of the other label switching proposals. Like the inventors of Tag Switching, the ARIS team has submitted a large number of Internet drafts to the IETF, and these are the main source of information for this chapter.

There is no doubt that Tag Switching and ARIS were invented in parallel—the announcement of ARIS followed that of Tag Switching by only a few weeks and was reported to have been ready well beforehand. Both proposals rely on some ideas that had been published previously, such as the notion of threaded indices described by Varghese in 1995. The naming of ARIS, Aggregate Route-based IP Switching, suggests something about its origins: unlike Ipsilon's IP Switching, ARIS binds labels to aggregate routes (or groups of address prefixes), rather than to flows.

There are many significant differences between ARIS and Tag Switching in spite of their architectural similarity. We will discuss these differences and their impact in Chapter 7. In this chapter, we begin with an overview of what functionality ARIS provides and how it works. We then describe how ARIS deals with both ATM and shared medial LAN links. Finally, we examine the details of the ARIS protocol, which provides the label binding capability for this approach. In some areas, ARIS and Tag Switching are so similar that it would be redundant to describe a feature in this chapter that has already been covered in Chapter 5. For this reason, it is important that this chapter be read after Chapter 5.

6.1 ARIS Overview

In the taxonomy of Chapter 2, ARIS is a control-driven approach, just like Tag Switching. Thus, it sets up label bindings and label switched paths in response to control traffic, such as routing updates. Routers and switches that are able to participate in label switching (which we have called Label Switching Routers (LSRs) in this book) are referred to as Integrated Switch Routers (ISRs).

The developers of ARIS have focused considerable energy on the issues that arise when the ARIS routers are implemented using ATM switching hardware. This focus is reflected in more detailed specifications for the ATM case and less detail on the operation over frame-based media. In most of this section we will describe the case where ISRs communicate over point-to-point links, which may be either frame-based or ATM links. Sections 6.2 and 6.3 add detail for the special case of ATM links and shared media links, respectively.

We begin the discussion of ARIS by looking at how it provides the most basic sort of label switching functionality, destination-based routing. We will then move on to discuss additional functions that can be supported.

6.1.1 *Destination-Based Routing*

To understand how ARIS supports destination-based routing, we first need to introduce the ARIS concept of *egress identifiers* or egress IDs. To explain this concept, we consider the example network in Figure 6.1. In this figure, there is a region (shown as a gray oval) in which label switched paths can be created. This region is bounded by Integrated Switch Routers, and all devices inside the region are also ISRs. If we consider a packet destined to conventional router B, coming from conventional router A, it would enter the ISR region at ISR X (the ingress ISR) and would leave the region at ISR Y (the egress ISR). A label switched path would be set up from X to Y. One might think that the egress ID associated with this path would be some identifier related to the egress ISR, and in many cases this would be correct. However, as the ARIS architecture has expanded to encompass more functionality, the definition of an egress ID has become broader as well. Thus we will see examples below where the egress ID identifies something other than the egress ISR. However, in the simple case that we consider first, an egress ID means just what we would expect: it identifies a particular egress ISR. Egress IDs must be unique within the label switching region. To ensure uniqueness of egress IDs, one could use the router IDs that are used in OSPF routing messages, which must be unique to enable the correct operation of OSPF.

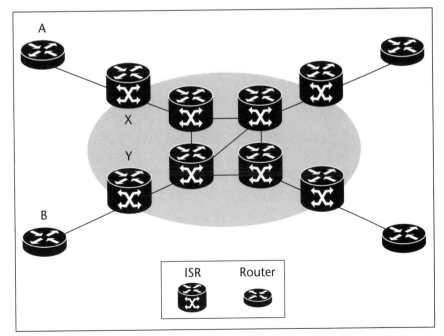

Figure 6.1 *Integrated Switch Routers and egress identifiers.*

The establishment of label switched paths for destination-based routing in the ARIS architecture is originated by the egress ISR. In the terminology of Chapter 2, this is a downstream allocation model. It is also an ordered (rather than independent) label creation model. We will see how these models work in practice by examining the steps by which a label switched path is established.

As with all label switching approaches, it is assumed that all LSRs are running conventional routing protocols. The operation of ARIS, and the usage of egress IDs in particular, is dependent on the type of routing protocol used. ARIS ISRs need to determine what type of egress ID is being used based on the routing protocol being used and perhaps some local configuration. We begin this discussion by assuming that a link-state protocol (such as OSPF) is being used, and furthermore that all the ISRs in the region in question (the gray region of Figure 6.1) are in the same routing area. The consequence of these assumptions is that all ISRs in the region have a complete database of the topology of the region. This in turn means that an ISR can determine not just the next hop for any entry in its routing table, but also the egress ISR for that entry. For example, looking back to Figure 6.1, ISR X might have some number of entries in its routing table for address prefixes that are reachable through ISR Y. ISR X would augment its routing table with the information that the egress router for those routes is ISR Y.

To begin the establishment of a label switched path, an egress ISR advertises a binding between a label and its own egress ID to its upstream ISR neighbors. As noted above, the egress ID must be unique to the network. The routers in a region all need to agree on how egress IDs are chosen. The upstream neighbors are, in the case of an egress ISR, all ISRs to which it is directly connected.

Upon receiving an advertisement from a neighboring ISR, the recipient ISR checks to see whether the message came from the expected next hop for that egress ID by checking the routing table entry for the route to the ISR with that egress ID. If the message did not come from the appropriate next hop, then it is discarded. (The recipient may also perform some loop prevention procedures, which are described in Section 6.1.3.) If the message did come from the appropriate next hop, then the ISR records the binding between the egress ID and the advertised label. It now knows that this label can be used as the outgoing label for all routes in its routing table that have that egress ID.

Once the ISR has processed the received message, it generates a new label binding between a locally assigned label and the egress ID of the received message. It stores this as the incoming label for those routes in the routing table that match the egress ID and then advertises the binding to its neighbors. Those neighbors in turn process the advertisement in exactly the same way, so that eventually the advertisement propagates all the way to the ingress of the ISR region. At this point, every ISR in the region that uses the egress ISR in question for any routes at all will have incoming and outgoing label bindings for those routes and can forward packets toward that egress ISR using label switching. We can see how this process works by means of an example (see Figure 6.2).

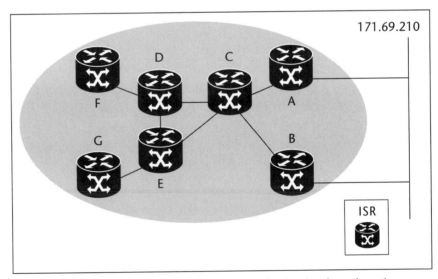

Figure 6.2 *Example of ARIS operation—destination-based routing.*

In the example network of Figure 6.2, the gray oval represents an area of interconnected ISRs. On the right is a network with the address prefix 171.69.210, which is connected to both ISR A and ISR B. Let's assume for this example that all the ISRs except ISR B have chosen a route to 171.69.210 that passes through ISR A. Thus, they all have a routing table entry for 171.69.210 that includes an egress ID corresponding to ISR A. For example, the routing table in ISR C (called the Forwarding Information Base in the ARIS documents) would have an entry like the following:

Prefix	Next hop	Egress ID
171.69.210	ISR A	ISR A

Assume that ISR A advertises a binding between its egress ID and a label. (ISR A will typically do this as soon as it learns that it has any neighbors who are ISRs, e.g., when it is booted or when it first establishes that it is connected to ISR C.) The binding advertisement message is called an ESTABLISH message in ARIS terminology. The first thing ISR C has to do when it receives the advertisement from A is to determine whether this message has arrived from the correct next hop. In this case, it is pretty obvious that A is the next hop for A, but in the general case, an ISR would check the routing table entry that corresponds to the router identified in the egress ID. For example, if ISR A had an IP address of 171.69.210.244, then C would look in its routing table to find the next hop for that address. It would, of course, be ISR A, so C would accept the message.

Suppose that the advertisement from A contains a binding between the label 17 and the egress ID for ISR A. Then ISR C would update its forwarding information base as follows:

Prefix	Next hop	Egress ID	Remote label
171.69.210	ISR A	ISR A	17

Note that when ISR B advertises bindings to ISR C, ISR C performs exactly the same steps. It first checks to see whether B is the next hop to B, which, of course, it is, and thus C decides to accept the message. It then looks to see whether ISR B is the egress router for any routes in its routing table. In this simple example, it may be that B is not the egress for any routes, so the message is discarded.

Having processed the advertisement from ISR A, ISR C creates a local label binding. Let's suppose it allocates the label 10. Although we could add that as another column to the table we've used so far, the ARIS documents talk about a separate table called the VC information base, or VCIB. (Note that the term *VC*, or virtual circuit, is used here to refer to a label switched path, which is not exactly the same as a conventional VC, notably because it may be multipoint-to-point.) The VCIB contains information that is used to forward label switched packets, which would include the incoming label, outgoing label, and outgoing interface.

ISR C now advertises a binding between the egress ID for ISR A and the label 10 to all of its neighbors except ISR A. ISR B, we may assume, does not believe that ISR C is the next hop toward ISR A, because B can reach A directly over the 171.69.210 network. Thus ISR B discards the advertisement. Both ISRs D and E, however, believe that C is the next hop to A, and so accept the advertisement. They process it just as C did, storing the label 10 as the outgoing label for routes corresponding to this egress ID and assigning new labels, which they in turn advertise to their neighbors.

When ISR F receives an advertisement from ISR D, it processes the message and stores the outgoing label provided by D. However, ISR F has no more ISR neighbors aside from D and thus does not need to assign a locally generated label or make any further advertisements.

It should be clear that the overall effect of the propagation of label assignments from egress to ingress is to build up a multipoint-to-point tree rooted at the egress. This is shown in Figure 6.3.

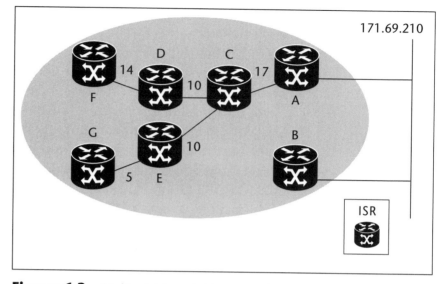

171.69.210

Figure 6.3 *Multipoint-to-point tree rooted at egress.*

Assuming that D advertised a label with the value 14 to F, then F will have a routing table entry as follows:

Prefix	Next hop	Egress ID	Remote label
171.69.210	ISR D	ISR A	14

When a data packet arrives at F from outside the ISR region, F applies the longest match algorithm to find the prefix that matches the packet. F is, in our terminology, a label edge router. A packet destined for network 171.69.210 will match the entry above. ISR F applies the label 14 to the packet and forwards it toward D, from which point it is label switched all the way to the egress. ISR D replaces the label 14 with 10 and forwards the packet toward ISR C; C replaces the label with 17 and forwards the packet toward ISR A; and ISR A removes the label before forwarding the packet onto the 171.69.210 network.

As we noted at the outset, this is a controlled approach to label distribution. It begins at the egress and propagates in an orderly fashion toward the ingress. This differs from the independent approach used in Tag Switching, in which any LSR can generate label bindings.

6.1.2 *Distance Vector Routing*

In the above discussion, it was assumed that every ISR could determine the ID of the egress router for any route in its routing table. Although this is possible when link-state routing is used, and may also be possible when entries in the routing table are derived from BGP, it is not possible when distance vector protocols (such as RIP and EIGRP) are used. This is because distance vector protocols do not provide a complete topological database to the routers; they only learn the correct next hop for each prefix. The consequence of this for ARIS is that a different sort of egress ID must be used, and potentially more labels must be assigned. The "egress identifier" no longer identifies an egress router; instead, it identifies a prefix carried in the DV protocol. An egress ISR will bind a label to that identifier and advertise it in an ESTABLISH message if it has a route to that prefix whose next hop is outside the ISR region.

To see how this works, consider the example of Figure 6.2. Both ISR A and ISR B will create a label binding for 171.69.210 and advertise it to ISR C. C, however, knows that A is the next hop to this "egress identifier" and thus disregards the message from B. The setup of the label switched path from ingress to egress proceeds pretty much as before. However, compared to the link-state case, potentially more labels will be assigned. In the first example, the addition of more networks that are reachable through ISR A will not cause any new label switched paths to be established. By contrast, with a DV protocol, every new prefix that is reachable through ISR A must be advertised as a new egress ID and a new label switched path will be set up.

It is worth noting that the relationship between number of labels assigned and type of routing used isn't really unique to ARIS, but exists in Tag Switching as well. However, it is more readily apparent in ARIS because of the use of egress IDs rather than prefixes in the label binding process.[1]

6.1.3 *Loop Prevention*

Up till now we have glossed over the ARIS loop prevention mechanism. We noted in Chapter 2 that transient forwarding loops are essentially a fact of life with IP routing protocols. They occur because, even though the routing protocols may try to ensure that all routers have a consistent view of the topology, the distribution of topological information and the calculation of routing tables takes a finite and not entirely predictable amount of time. Thus, it is always possible that, for a short period of time, router A thinks that the next hop to some route is router B, while B thinks that the next hop for the same route is A. (Normally the loops are a little more complex than this example.) Even though, in the absence of misconfiguration or implementation bugs, loops will go away as soon as routing reconverges, they can do considerable damage while they exist.

The tried-and-tested approach to handling transient forwarding loops in IP networks is the use of the TTL (time-to-live) field. This field is decremented at least once by every router that forwards a packet, so that a looping packet is eventually discarded before doing too much damage. It is important to discard looping packets so that the routers can focus on the important job of getting their routing tables stabilized and consistent again, rather than forwarding an ever-increasing number of packets caught in the loop. As we saw in the preceding chapter, the same approach can be made to work in a label switched network, but only if the LSR is able to perform a TTL decrement operation. When ATM switch hardware is used as an LSR, this is not an option, both because the hardware lacks the capability to decrement TTL at each hop and because there is nowhere to carry it in the ATM cell. Like IP

---

[1] Tag Switching, when performing destination-based routing, generally will assign the same number of label switched paths as ARIS. However, this is done by binding the same tag to different prefixes (which can be done in a single message) as opposed to a redefinition of the egress ID.

Switching, ARIS has a mechanism to adjust TTL at the ends of a label switched path instead of decrementing at each hop, which is described in the next section. It also has a means to prevent the establishment of a looping label switched path, which we examine now.

When an egress router advertises a binding between its ID and a label, it also initializes an entry in the advertisement message called the ISR path. The ISR path is the record of all the ISRs that have propagated the advertisement of this particular egress ID. The egress router puts its own ID in this field. As each ISR on the path from egress to ingress receives the advertisement and creates a binding for this egress ID and advertises it to its neighbors, it adds its own ID to the ISR path. Thus, if a transient routing loop causes the ESTABLISH messages to follow a loop, it will be detected, because an ISR will see its own ID in the ISR path. When detected, the process of propagating bindings back toward the ingress is halted. This ensures that a looping switched path can never be set up.

The approach just described to loop prevention is superficially similar to that used by BGP with AS paths. However, with BGP the AS path is actually used to prevent the looping of *routing* information, while in ARIS the motivation is to prevent *forwarding* loops. The granularity is also very different: BGP uses lists of Autonomous Systems (AS) and ARIS uses lists of individual routers. In summary, one should not extrapolate from the experience of BGP to analyze the ARIS approach.

6.1.4 *TTL Adjustment*

Although the decrementing of TTL is important in mitigating the effects of transient forwarding loops, it has a variety of other uses. For example, it is also used by various tools, most notably traceroute, to determine the hops along an IP path. Because label switching routers provide control functionality equivalent to IP routers, it can be argued that they need to support tools that depend on TTL in the same way. For those LSRs that do not decrement TTL as part of their normal forwarding (e.g., those based on ATM hardware) some alternate mechanism is needed. ARIS provides such a mechanism.

We can divide the TTL problem into two parts. The first is making sure that TTL is decremented by the correct number of hops when a packet traverses an ISR region. The second is making sure that a packet whose TTL is so low that it will expire inside an ISR cloud is delivered to the processor at the last ISR on its path. This latter is needed to support traceroute, which depends on the return of ICMP messages from routers at which a packet's TTL has expired.

The solution to the first part of the problem is rather straightforward. By the time an ESTABLISH message has propagated from the egress ISR to the ingress, it has collected a list of all the hops in the path, as described above. Thus, it is easy for the ingress ISR to decrement the TTL of an arriving packet by the number of hops that it will traverse across the ISR region before sending it on its label switched path.

But what if a packet turns up at an ingress ISR and the TTL is less than the number of hops to get across the ISR region? This packet's TTL will expire at some point as it traverses the region. To get it to the correct point of expiry (i.e., the router at which its TTL would expire if all ISRs were decrementing TTL by one), ARIS permits the ingress ISR to forward the packet hop by hop. That is, it is not sent on a label switched path at all. Instead, it is sent to the next hop ISR using a VC that terminates in the control processor of the ISR, like the default VC used by CSRs and IP Switches. On receiving the packet, the ISR performs a full layer 3 lookup, including TTL decrement. It is then sent to the control processor of the next hop ISR, again using a default VC. In hop by hop mode, each ISR behaves like a conventional router, complete with TTL decrementing, and can thus discard a packet if the TTL reaches zero and generate the response on which traceroute depends.

While this approach certainly maintains the expected behavior from the traceroute tool, it has some undesirable effects on behavior during routing transients, as we discuss below.

6.1.5 *Behavior During Routing Transients*

It is worth considering what would happen in the event of a change in routing information. We return again to the example of Figure 6.2. Suppose, for example, that the cost of the link from D to C were increased so that the best route from D to the egress ISR A was via ISR E. D would have to stop using the switched path that goes via C and would request a label from ISR E using a TRIGGER message. The TRIGGER message requests a binding for the egress ID that corresponds to ISR A. E creates a binding between the egress ID and a locally assigned label and conveys this information to D in an ESTABLISH message.

When D receives the ESTABLISH message, it checks to see whether the path is loop free. If so, it appends its own ISR ID to the path, creates a new label binding for this egress ID, and sends a new ESTABLISH message to ISR F. ISR F replaces the old label binding with the new one, updates its tables accordingly, and the new path is established.

It is important to realize that while this process is going on, there are periods of time when an ISR does not have a switched path to the egress ISR. This may happen just because of the time it takes to receive a response to a TRIGGER message. But it may last even longer, because there is a possibility that the ESTABLISH message received in response to the trigger might contain a loop. After all, loops occur during routing transients, which was the reason for the trigger event. Note that the loss of a switched path occurs as the result of a topology change, not necessarily the formation of a loop. Thus we see the first problem of loop prevention: it is almost unavoidable that a loop prevention scheme will affect traffic that was not on a looping path. Exactly how it is affected depends on what steps we take when the switched path is broken.

When an ISR does not have a viable switched path for a certain egress ID, the ARIS specification permits (but does not require) the ISR to forward packets for that ID hop by hop; that is, they are sent directly to the next hop ISR, which must process them using conventional layer 3 forwarding, including TTL processing. The only feasible alternative is to drop the packets. Note that these packets may not be in any danger of looping. Nevertheless, dropping packets may still be preferable to hop by hop forwarding.

If hop by hop forwarding is used during routing transients, it is worth noting that this potentially places an additional burden on that part of the ISR that is able to perform full layer 3 forwarding. In many implementations, this is likely to be the same processor that processes routing updates. It is almost certain to be slower than the label switched forwarding path. Clearly it is risky to increase the packet forwarding load on the processing engine of a router at exactly the point in time when it most needs to focus on processing routing updates. This behavior has the potential to further increase the amount of time it takes for routing to reconverge, making matters worse. Note the difference between the ISR and a conventional router in this case. A conventional router does not change the way it forwards data packets during routing transients, whereas the ISR actually moves a portion of the data packets out of the label switched path into the control processor for forwarding during transients, thus increasing the forwarding load on the processor at the exact time when it most needs to be dedicated to processing routing messages. We return to this issue in Section 7.4.1.

6.1.6 *Additional ARIS Capabilities*

Explicit Routes

ARIS provides support for explicit routes through the use of a new type of egress ID. An Explicit Route Object can be carried in an ESTABLISH message to bind labels to the explicit route. This works pretty much the same as in the previous example, in which a label was bound to the path to the egress router that was determined by IP routing. With explicit routes, the label is bound to an explicitly specified route.

The Explicit Route Object is just a list of IP addresses of the hops that must be traversed. It is a strict source route, in the sense that no additional hops may be present between the specified hops. It is possible for the establishment of an explicitly routed path to begin at the egress or ingress to an ISR region, in contrast to the examples we have seen so far, which were always initiated by the egress.

Multicast

It may come as no surprise to find that ARIS supports multicast by defining yet another type of "egress identifier" and binding labels to those identifiers. Of course an egress ID in no way represents an egress router in this case, since the multicast trees to which labels are bound have multiple egresses from the ISR region.

Consistent with the overall approach of ARIS, the binding of labels for multicast is handled using the ARIS protocol rather than piggybacking on top of multicast routing protocols. This in principle should allow all multicast routing protocols to be supported, although the details have not been clearly spelled out at the time of writing. The basic idea, however, is simple enough: ARIS ESTAB-LISH messages can be used to advertise bindings between labels and multicast trees. Trees may be shared among all senders to a group or may be sender specific; ARIS allows labels to be bound to either type of tree.

It is noticeable that the specifications for ARIS do not explain how to handle the problem of label assignment to multicast trees on shared media. In general the multicast portion of ARIS is not at the same level of completeness as the unicast case (or the Tag Switching treatment of multicast) at the time of writing.

RSVP

The binding of labels to RSVP reservations is the one situation in which the ARIS architecture piggybacks on an existing protocol rather than supplying the functionality in the ARIS protocol itself. The decision to use RSVP for the distribution of bindings can perhaps be explained by the fact that there is only one RSVP. Thus, whereas piggybacking label distribution on a unicast routing protocol, for example, would imply the need to modify several protocols just to get one piece of functionality, RSVP is the only resource reservation protocol that needs to be modified to get resource reservation functionality. Furthermore, as we noted previously, the structure of RSVP naturally lends itself to label binding distribution. This natural structure caused both the ARIS and Tag Switching design teams to make similar design decisions. In fact, there is so little difference between the two approaches that we refer the reader to Section 5.1.4 for discussion of the mechanics of label binding distribution in RSVP.

Tunnels

The ARIS proposal allows nested label switched paths to be built. In the ARIS terminology, such paths are called *L2 (layer 2) tunnels*. To illustrate how L2 tunnels work, consider the network of ISRs shown in Figure 6.4.

If we consider packets flowing from left to right in the figure in the absence of L2 tunnels, there are four label switched paths: (X, A, B, C, Y), (X, A, B, C, V), (W, A, B, C, Y), and (W, A, B, C, V). The following procedures may be used to establish an L2 tunnel from A to C. Both Y and V advertise their egress IDs, together with the associated labels to C. C is configured as an egress of the L2 tunnel. So, rather than creating bindings for these IDs and propagating the IDs and the bindings to B, C places these IDs and the labels into the Tunnel Object and passes this information to B in the ESTABLISH message. The message, in addition to the Tunnel Object, contains the egress ID of C, as well as the binding that C associates with this egress ID.

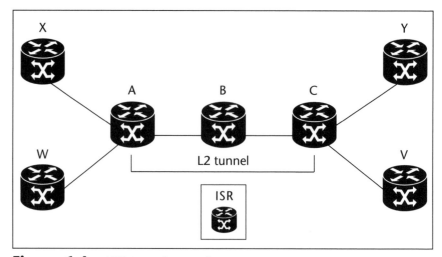

Figure 6.4   *ARIS tunnel example.*

When B receives the ESTABLISH message from C, B doesn't create any labels associated with Y or V. However, when sending an ESTABLISH message with C's egress identifier to A, B also includes in the message the Tunnel Object that it received from C. This object contains the egress IDs and labels of Y and V. Because A is configured as an ingress to the L2 tunnel, when A receives the ESTABLISH message from B, A extracts the egress identifiers and the labels for Y and V carried in the Tunnel Object, creates bindings for these identifiers, and advertises these bindings to X and W.

Consider packets flowing from X to Y once the tunnel has been set up in this way. A packet transmitted by X will be labeled with the label that ISR A bound to the egress ID for Y. At ISR A, the label is replaced by the one that was carried in the Tunnel Object. Then the label that B advertised is pushed onto the label stack. That label is swapped as the packet is forwarded at B, and then ISR C pops the label stack to reveal the labels that will be used to forward the packet to ISR Y. Note that ISR B thus has no forwarding state associated with ISRs Y and V.

6.2 ATM Issues

As noted above, the designers of ARIS have focused quite heavily on ATM as the link layer for deployment of the architecture. The focus on loop prevention is an example of an area where the details of ATM (in this case, the lack of a TTL field in the cell) has driven the design. There are some ATM-specific issues that remain to be covered, primarily related to the fact that ATM switches forward cells rather than frames.

As we discussed in the previous chapter, the behavior of conventional ATM hardware provides some challenges for label switching approaches that assign labels in such a way that packets from different sources can traverse the same link with the same label. This is only a problem for ARIS and Tag Switching because, unlike IP Switching and CSR, they can assign labels based on the destination of a packet only. ARIS is able to use the same options as Tag Switching to deal with this problem: VC-merge and assignment of multiple labels. These were described in detail in Section 5.2.2. There is yet another approach (which could also be applied to Tag Switching, but which has been documented only by the ARIS team), called VP-merge, which we describe here. The process of assigning multiple labels in ARIS when neither VC-merge nor VP-merge is supported is described at the end of this section.

6.2.1 *VP-Merge*

In this approach, the label is carried only in the VPI field of the ATM cells. The VCI field is then used as an identifier to distinguish frames that came from different sources but are being sent on the same link with the same label in the VPI field. This is illustrated in Figure 6.5. In this figure, the VPI is shown to the left of the VCI in each cell. The switch forwards based on the VPI and rewrites the VPI value, just like a conventional VP switch. However, because the two incoming streams of cells have different VCI values, which are not modified by the switch, there is no confusion between cells from different frames on the outgoing link.

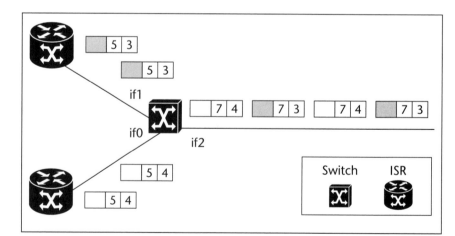

Figure 6.5   *VP-merge example.*

This approach does have its drawbacks. First, it limits the number of labels to the size of the VPI space, which is at most 12 bits. Second, it requires a unique 16-bit identifier to be assigned to each ingress ISR, which requires some degree of extra administration and configuration. Finally, the majority of existing switch hardware cannot perform Early or Partial Packet Discard (EPD or PPD) when switching on the VPI only. These features aim to discard whole frames (or the tail end of a frame in the case of PPD) once it is necessary to drop a single cell from the frame, since the rest of the frame is rendered useless by the single cell loss. They are valuable in reducing congestion and improving overall network throughput.

6.2.2 *Non-Merging Switches*

When neither VC-merge nor VP-merge is available, there needs to be some mechanism to allocate labels such that cell interleave does not interfere with the correct reception of frames. This is done by increasing the number of labels that are allocated on each link in such a way that frames from different sources are differentiated. ARIS does this by modifying the label allocation process.

Recall that ESTABLISH messages carry label bindings from egress ISRs toward ingress ISRs. When the ISR region contains ATM switches that cannot perform merging, a modified ESTABLISH message is used that causes label binding to flow from ingress to egress. This enables the establishment of one label per ingress/ egress pair, which is necessary to prevent cell interleave.

The technique works as follows: an egress ISR that is connected to nonmerging ISRs does not allocate a label but instead sends an ESTABLISH message with no label and an "end-to-end" bit, which says, in effect, that the label allocation should begin at the ingress. This message is forwarded back toward the ingress ISRs just as before, working its way backward along a multipoint-to-point tree. On reaching the ingress ISR, a label is allocated and placed in an ACKNOWLEDGE message, which is then sent toward the egress ISR. Each intermediate ISR allocates a new label and forwards the acknowledgment toward the egress. The effect is to create a *point-to-point* label switched path from every ingress to the egress.

Looking back to the earlier example, which is reproduced in Figure 6.6, we can see that an ESTABLISH message from ISR A will eventually propagate back to ISRs F and G. They will then allocate labels, which they bind to the egress ID for ISR A. When both D and E forward the acknowledgment to ISR C, C allocates a label per acknowledgment and sends two bindings on toward ISR A. Thus we end up with a pair of labels bound to the egress ID for ISR A on the link C-A, which is what is required to ensure that frames sent from ISR F can be distinguished from those sent by ISR G.

Note that this scheme actually uses *upstream* allocation of labels, as defined in Chapter 2. The node that assigns a label is the sender of data bearing that label; that is, it is at the upstream end of the link. Because there is still only one assigner of labels on a link, there is no risk of conflicting assignments, as long as there is not some other process assigning labels at the downstream end.

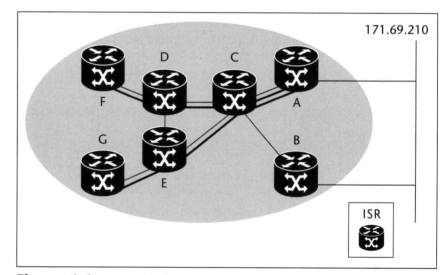

Figure 6.6   *Example of nonmerging ISRs. Bold lines indicate label switched paths.*

6.3 Label Encapsulation

ARIS has so far produced two methods for carrying labels, one for ATM and one for shared media LANs. There is no encapsulation defined for point-to-point media other than ATM (e.g., PPP links). There is nothing very remarkable about the way ARIS carries labels in ATM. As in every other approach, the label must be placed where an ATM switch can use it, that is, in the VCI or VPI field.

ARIS's LAN encapsulation is very different from the Tag Switching approach (the only other approach that has a LAN encapsulation). The ARIS team has proposed carrying the label inside the destination address field of the MAC header. The stated goal is to allow existing LAN switching hardware to function as an ISR. However, there are some significant problems to overcome with such an approach, as described below.

The ARIS proposal puts the label inside the destination address field of the MAC header, as shown in Figure 6.7. The first 24 bits are a standard Ethernet OUI (organizationally unique identifier), which indicates that this in fact is not a normal MAC address but a label. The next 20 bits are the actual label, followed by 3 bits of Class of Service and a stack bit. The COS bits enable packets to receive different "class of service" treatment in the network and are similar to the precedence field in the IP header. The stack bit is used to enable multiple tags, when hierarchical tags are used. Note that the encapsulation has no TTL field, which means that this encapsulation brings with it all the looping and TTL adjustment issues of the ATM encapsulation. The mechanisms that are applied to ATM ISRs can be applied here also, but loop mitigation using TTL cannot.

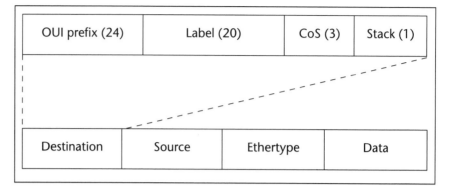

Figure 6.7   *ARIS label encapsulation for LAN media.*

The first thing to notice about this encapsulation is that it enables an LSR to attach a label to a packet without affecting its length. This would be a good thing in the case where an edge LSR was receiving unlabeled packets whose length equaled the MTU (maximum transmission unit) for the LAN in question. It would be able to add a label to such packets without increasing their length, thus staying within the MTU requirements. By contrast, an encapsulation that increased the length would require the edge LSR either to perform fragmentation of the packet or to send a packet that was too large. However, if hierarchical tags are used, then the length would still be increased with the ARIS encapsulation.

A notable characteristic of this approach is that it puts the label in a place where an existing piece of hardware, such as a LAN switch, might expect to find it. This is, in some sense, analogous to putting labels in the VCI field of an ATM switch. The problem with the analogy is that ATM switches are label swapping devices and LAN switches are not. Thus, whereas putting labels in the VCI field of an ATM cell leverages the capabilities of existing switch hardware, the same claim cannot be made for this LAN encapsulation. Any device that is to act as an LSR using this encapsulation will need to have label switching capability that is not available in any existing LAN switching hardware.

One might expect that the ARIS LAN encapsulation might be able to utilize existing router hardware, but this turns out not to be the case. The problem is that an ISR might in principle receive a packet with any value in the destination address. Devices that are able to receive such a range of packets are said to operate in *promiscuous* mode. Conventional bridges, for example, operate in this mode. However, we have already seen that conventional bridges do not perform label swapping, so they cannot fulfill the role of an ISR. Making a host or router operate in promiscuous mode is costly—sometimes prohibitively so—because it needs to receive every packet that arrives at its network interface card and decide (usually in software) whether the packet is relevant to the recipient or not. Thus, neither standard router hardware nor standard bridge hardware can easily use this encapsulation.

Another potentially significant issue with this scheme arises when we consider how label switching might be deployed. When deploying LSRs in a WAN environment, one only needs to replace the two devices at the ends of a link (or perhaps install some new software) to enable label switching across that link. All the schemes described so far can be deployed in a reasonably incremental fashion. As we noted in Chapter 3, a strength of the Toshiba CSR scheme is that it can even be deployed when CSRs communicate over a switched virtual circuit offered by a public carrier. However, in the LAN environment, which is clearly the environment in which this encapsulation will be used, deployment issues are different. In particular, the link between a pair of routers usually contains numerous bridges and LAN switches. It will often be desirable to be able to upgrade the routers to label switches without having to worry about any bridges or LAN switches that are between the routers. Such incremental deployment is more difficult when labels are carried in the MAC header, for reasons we now describe.

Consider what happens if a pair of ISRs using this encapsulation attempt to communicate over a LAN that includes some bridges or switches. These devices expect the address fields in the MAC header to have a particular meaning, which is different from that used by the ARIS scheme. To deal with this, the ARIS ESTABLISH messages that advertise a binding to a certain label place that label in the *source address* field of the message. By doing this, the bridges and switches are fooled into thinking that a device with that address is located where the advertising ISR is. They will thus forward packets containing that label in the *destination* address field toward the advertising LSR.

Because ISRs are in effect creating MAC addresses on-the-fly each time they advertise a new binding, care needs to be taken to make sure that two ISRs on the same LAN do not allocate the same label at the same time. This is different from the ATM-LSR case, where all links are point-to-point; it also differs from the LAN encapsulation used by Tag Switching, where the uniqueness of a label is assured by the fact that it is carried in a frame with the real MAC addresses of sender and receiver. The ARIS approach deals with the problem by partitioning the label space among all the ISRs on a LAN, using either static or dynamic means (which are not yet specified at the time of writing). Such partitioning is likely to be administratively complex.

Another potential problem for bridges in this environment is that the dynamic allocation of labels may create many more MAC addresses for the bridges to store in their tables than they are designed to handle. When these tables overflow, excessive flooding of packets can occur on the LAN.

Thus, there are serious difficulties to using this scheme with either existing bridge hardware or with existing devices such as routers. It seems unlikely that the encapsulation described here will be widely deployed.

6.4 The ARIS Protocol

This section provides a snapshot of the ARIS protocol, based on the Internet drafts available at the time of writing. It is reasonable to expect that future revisions to the protocol, if they are produced, will add further functionality to that described here rather than making significant changes to the overall operation of the protocol. This section is intended to give some insights into the nuts and bolts of the protocol that are not apparent just from looking at the ARIS architecture.

6.4.1 *Protocol Structure*

The ARIS protocol contains a number of main message types (such as ESTABLISH, TRIGGER, etc.), the details of which are described below. Messages are sent directly on top of IP and are identified by the protocol number in the IP header (the value used by ARIS is 104). Each message begins with a common header, which includes a field specifying what type of message this is. The format of the common header is shown in Figure 6.8.

Most of the fields are reasonably self-explanatory. A neighboring pair of ARIS routers establish a session, which is identified by a session number; the messages that are sent are identified by sequence numbers. The reason for using sequence numbers is that the ARIS label binding protocol runs directly over IP—it does not rely on an underlying reliable byte stream protocol such as TCP to provide reliability or in-order delivery, both of which are needed in some circumstances. Thus, ARIS must provide its own reliability mechanisms in the label binding protocol. This is a design choice with significant consequences, which are discussed in Chapter 7.

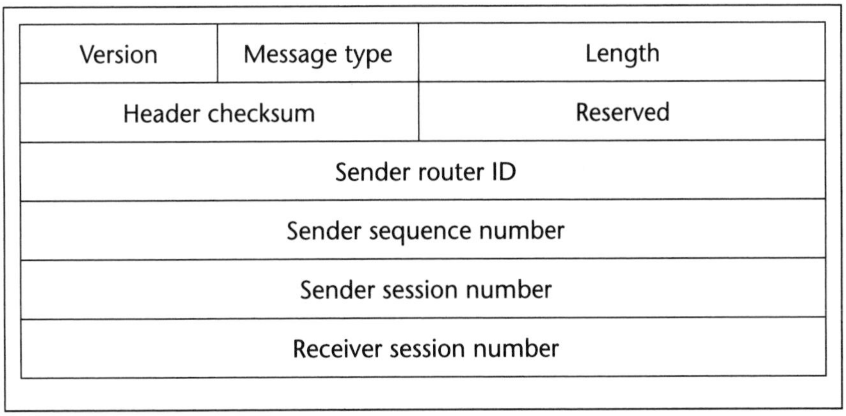

Version	Message type	Length
Header checksum		Reserved
Sender router ID		
Sender sequence number		
Sender session number		
Receiver session number		

Figure 6.1 *The ARIS common header.*

Depending on the message type, the common header is followed by some number of objects. For example, there are object types for egress IDs and labels that are used in ESTABLISH messages. The ARIS protocol specification consists largely of the definitions of the various types of objects and the specification of which objects are required or allowed for each message type. We examine the main message types and the associated objects below.

6.4.2 *Protocol Operation*

The ARIS protocol runs between a pair of ISRs, which are normally directly connected neighbors. The process begins with an ISR sending an INIT message to one of its directly connected neighbors. As well as letting the neighbor know that this ISR exists, the INIT message carries information about the capabilities of the ISR, such as the range of labels that it can support and the time-out period that it wishes to use. The recipient of the message replies with an INIT message and, if all goes well, an adjacency is established. In the absence of any other information flow, the two parties have to send KEEPALIVE messages periodically to keep the adjacency up.

Once the adjacency is established, the parties may send each other various types of messages to do with the creation, modification, and deletion of bindings between labels and egress IDs. The major message types are ESTABLISH, ACK, TRIGGER, and TEAR. We shall see how each is used below.

An ESTABLISH message, as already discussed, establishes a binding between an egress ID and a label. It also contains a list of routers that have been traversed in getting the binding from the egress ISR to the current point. The recipient of an ESTABLISH message checks to see whether

- the message came from the next hop toward the route or device described by the egress ID
- the path that the message has traversed up to this point is loop free (i.e., does not contain the same ISR twice)

If both conditions hold, then the recipient responds with an ACKNOWLEDGMENT (ACK) message to the sender. It will also create a new ESTABLISH message to send to its other neighbors, after first allocating a new label and adding itself to the list of ISRs traversed by the message. Note that the sender of the ESTABLISH message must receive either a positive or negative acknowledgment (even if the binding is going to be ignored for failing to meet the conditions above) or it will keep retransmitting the message. A negative acknowledgment can be used to indicate that the message was received but generated some sort of error.

Note that the use of ACK messages is required in ARIS because it runs directly over IP. This contrasts with the tag (label) distribution protocol used by Tag Switching, which uses the built-in reliable delivery mechanisms of TCP.

TRIGGER messages are used to explicitly request a new binding rather than waiting for the next ESTABLISH message to arrive. A TRIGGER is used if a routing change causes the next hop toward some egress ID to change; the upstream node sends the TRIGGER message toward the new next hop, which should respond with an ESTABLISH message. Processing of this message is essentially the same as above.

The TEARDOWN (TEAR) message is effectively the opposite of an ESTABLISH message—it enables an egress ISR to withdraw bindings that it had previously advertised. One reason to do this might be if an egress ISR stopped being an egress ISR because it no longer has any non-ARIS neighbors. The teardown message would follow the same path as the ESTABLISH message for the bindings it needs to remove, and all the ISRs along that path would release the appropriate label bindings.

6.5 Summary

The ARIS approach to label switching, like Tag Switching, is a control-driven approach, which creates label bindings in response to control traffic, when the routing protocols determine reachability to an address prefix, for example. In most cases, the establishment of a label switched path is initiated by the egress Integrated Switch Router (ISR), which is the last ISR on the path. The establishment of a label binding propagates from egress toward the ingress ISRs in a region of interconnected ISRs, setting up label switched paths in an orderly way.

To deal with the lack of a TTL field in ATM cells, ARIS enables loop prevention by carrying a list of all the routers traversed by an ESTABLISH message. More than one appearance of any router in the list is an indication of a possible loop, and the label switched path will not be established.

One of the key concepts of ARIS is the egress identifier (egress ID). In the simplest case, an egress ID represents the identity of the ISR at the egress end of a label switched path. However, the term is more of a catchall for anything that might have a label switched path associated with it. Thus, an egress ID might represent any number of things, such as a prefix carried in a distance vector protocol or a multicast tree. Extending the notion of an egress ID beyond its obvious meaning has enabled the architecture to grow to encompass many features and capabilities such as multicast, explicit routes, and resource reservations. It does, however, mean that the name itself is somewhat misleading.

In addition to the obvious label encapsulation for ATM, in which labels are carried in the VCI or VPI field, the ARIS team has developed a LAN encapsulation that places labels in the destination field of the MAC header. Although it avoids fragmentation issues, the approach raises some problems of label space allocation and the need to operate LAN interfaces in promiscuous mode.

The ARIS protocol is a peer-to-peer protocol that runs between ISRs directly over IP. The protocol includes an initialization phase, in which peers determine their neighbors' capabilities and establish an adjacency, followed by the active phase in which label bindings may be exchanged, requested, and deleted. Because it runs directly over IP, the protocol requires its own reliability mechanisms.

Further Reading

There are at the time of writing no archival documents describing ARIS. The reader is encouraged to seek out the latest ARIS or MPLS-related Internet drafts. These are stored at many sites, including

ftp://ftp.isi.edu/internet-drafts

There is also an ARIS Website at

www.networking.ibm.com/nsw/aris.html

We recommend the first of the two references below as a piece of interesting historical background. The paper presents several techniques to improve router performance, including the notion of threaded indices, which is similar to the basic idea behind destination-based routing in both ARIS and Tag Switching. The second reference is provided for those who wish to look more closely at the issues involved in making LAN switches function as label switches; it provides good background on the operation of conventional bridges and LAN switches.

Chandranmenon, C., and G. Varghese. "Trading Packet Headers for Packet Processing." In Proceedings of ACM SIGCOMM 95, September 1995, 162–173.

Perlman, R. *Interconnections: Bridges and Routers*. Reading, MA: Addison-Wesley, 1992.

Chapter

7

Comparison of Label Switching Approaches

In this chapter we will examine the major differences between the four approaches to label switching covered in the previous chapters. We begin by reexamining the taxonomy that was introduced in Chapter 2 and seeing where each of the approaches sits in that taxonomy. Then we endeavor to evaluate the consequences of the most important design decisions made by the inventors of each approach. By far the most significant design choice is between a data-driven (or flow-driven) model and a control-driven model. After looking at the effects of that design choice, we look at the significant differences between the approaches in the data-driven and control-driven camps.

After comparing the various label switching techniques, we briefly compare the overall label switching approach with more conventional methods of forwarding IP packets. Because there are several new products that provide high performance IP forwarding without the use of label switching, it is reasonable to ask what benefits, if any, label switching offers over these approaches.

7.1 Taxonomy

In Table 7.1 we have classified the four label switching approaches described in this book in terms of the fundamental design decisions that were discussed in Chapter 2, such as the type of binding distribution. In Table 7.2, we list the features and functionality that the designers have chosen to support.

Because the data-driven versus control-driven design choice is such an important one, we devote the next section to a discussion of that choice and its consequences. In addition, it is easiest to make meaningful comparison of other factors in the context of either data-driven or control-driven approaches, and thus we discuss the different approaches in the two main classes in Sections 7.3 and 7.4.

Table 7.1   Architectural comparison of label switching approaches.

	CSR	IP Switching	Tag Switching	ARIS
Data- or control-driven	Data-driven	Data-driven	Control-driven	Control-driven
Loop prevention	Unspecified	Supported	Supported on ATM only	Supported on all media
Binding distribution	Upstream	Downstream	Downstream	Downstream
Binding creation	Independent	Independent	Independent (except explicit routes)	Ordered (from egress)
Label distribution protocol	Separate	Separate	Piggybacked/ separate	Separate (except RSVP)
Soft or hard state	Soft	Soft	Hard/soft	Soft

Table 7.2 Feature comparison of label switching approaches.

	CSR	IP Switching	Tag Switching	ARIS
Supported link types	ATM	ATM	ATM, PPP, Ethernet	ATM, Ethernet
Explicit route support	No	No	Yes	Yes
Multicast	Unspecified	Yes	Yes	Partial
Hierarchy of labels	No	No	Yes	Yes
Spoofing protection	No	Yes	No	No
ATM SVC interworking	Yes	No	No	No
Host support	No	Yes	Only RSVP	Only RSVP
RSVP	Yes	Yes	Yes	Yes

7.2 Control-Driven Versus Data-Driven Approaches

Recall that a control-driven approach creates label bindings in response to the arrival of control traffic, such as routing updates or resource reservation messages. By contrast, data-driven approaches look at the arriving patterns of data and decide based on that traffic whether to establish a label binding for some class of data packets. The choice between these methods for establishing bindings will clearly have some impact on performance and scalability, that is, how well the approach works as networks grow. We might also expect to see some effect on robustness, in the sense of how well the approach works in widely different conditions. We will discuss each of these areas of impact in turn.

7.2.1 *Performance*

The first thing to notice about the performance of various label switching schemes is that, under ideal conditions, all of the schemes can forward data at whatever speed label switching runs. In many cases, this is determined by the speed of the underlying hardware. Thus, for example, if a label switching scheme runs on an ATM switch, then the *best case* forwarding performance will be that of the ATM switch. Most ATM switches can forward traffic at "wire speed" on all of their interfaces, provided the traffic pattern is such that no interface is congested. Thus, for example, a 16 OC-3 port switch will have a capacity close to 16×155 Mbps = 2.5 Gbps. Under ideal conditions, any label switching scheme using this switch would achieve the same throughput.

The key phrase here is "under ideal conditions." The question is how close to ideal will the real operating environment be. This question has proven quite difficult to answer, especially for data-driven schemes. The ideal conditions for a data-driven scheme are when all flows are infinitely long-lived. In this case, the cost of setting up a label switched path for a flow is amortized over the (infinite) length of the flow, becoming negligible.

Considerable research has been performed to determine how far from ideal the conditions in real networks are. Part of the challenge of such research is finding reasonable traffic statistics, since most network operators are not very keen on making the details of their traffic traces publicly available. Furthermore, even when one can get real trace data, there are no guarantees that it will accurately reflect a "typical" network at the time it was collected, much less that it is an accurate predictor of the sort of traffic that will be found in networks in the near future.

The major performance issue for data-driven schemes when conditions deviate from ideal is the fact that every packet that is not label switched must be handled by the control processor (e.g., the IP Switch controller). This device is just a conventional router implemented in software, augmented by the flow detection code and a label distribution protocol. Almost by definition, it has much less forwarding capacity than the label switching hardware;

otherwise, why bother with label switching? So the concern is how much load can be placed on this device, especially considering the fact that it needs to run routing protocols as well.

If the control processor were very aggressive in selecting flows for label switching, it might be able to get away with forwarding only one packet per flow. Because of the adverse impact this would have on scalability (as we discuss below), plus the delay associated with setting up bindings at remote switches, it is much more likely to forward several packets at the start of each flow. We can conclude that the packet forwarding capacity that is required of the control processor is dependent on the rate at which new flows arrive and the number of packets in each flow that are not label switched. The rate of flow arrival equals the offered load in packets per second divided by the average number of packets per flow.

PPS required = (Packets forwarded per flow) × (PPS offered) / (Packets per flow)

The hard part of this to get a handle on is the packets forwarded per flow. Even if the flow identifier has a simple rule such as "Label switch any flow longer than 10 packets," there may be many flows that are only 1 packet long, which puts much less load on the control processor than flows that are 9 packets long. A number of papers (which appear in the Further Reading section of Chapter 4) have tried to address this issue. Note that the packet forwarding capacity of the control processor is crucial to the performance of data-driven schemes. If the processor is unable to keep up with the packet forwarding, flow classification, routing, and label binding work that is required, something has to give: either it drops data packets, stops doing flow identification and label distribution (which only makes matters worse), or stops processing routing updates (which could make matters much worse).

The consensus of the research is that performance of data-driven schemes under real traffic loads can be quite good, with a high fraction (70–80%) of the traffic label switched and thus achieving the performance of the underlying hardware. Ipsilon has also taken the issue of control processor performance seriously, making sure that it is adequate under relatively high load.[1] The main concerns with data-driven approaches are really scalability and robustness in the face of changing traffic patterns, subjects we will return to shortly.

Another performance issue that arises with data-driven schemes (and, to a lesser extent, with control-driven ones as well) is the "circuit setup rate." Every time an LSR decides that a flow should be label switched, it needs to exchange some signalling messages with its neighbors, and it may also need to make some changes to the state of its switching hardware (e.g., setting cross points in an ATM switch). All of these things consume CPU resources, and they consume more as a higher percentage of flows are selected to be label switched. It is hard to quantify how expensive the operation of setting up a flow is, but it is clear that the performance of data-driven schemes is sensitive to this factor. If the control processor cannot set up flows at the rate required by the flow detection algorithm, then a lower percentage of flows will have to be label switched, and performance will suffer.

What about control-driven schemes? Like data-driven schemes, they too can perform at the level of the underlying hardware under ideal conditions, but the definition of ideal is very different. For example, when providing destination-based routing functionality, the ideal conditions for a control-driven scheme are simple: as long as the topology is stable, all traffic that arrives at a (non-edge) LSR can be label switched without a single packet having to pass through the control processor. Unlike the data-driven schemes, one can imagine networks in which these ideal conditions might prevail for long periods.

When topology changes, it still may be possible for control-driven schemes to achieve ideal performance. Recall that a control-driven scheme may learn bindings for routes from neighbors who were not next hops for those routes; in the event of a topology

---

[1] A piece of Ipsilon folklore that we believe to be accurate is that founder Tom Lyon promised to shave his head if the engineers could get the control processor to forward IP packets at 150,000 packets per second. They met the challenge, and he delivered on his promise.

change making those neighbors become next hops, label switching can continue uninterrupted. (It is possible that, on some hardware platforms, a few packets might be lost while the label switching tables are modified; this is highly implementation dependent.) The behavior of Tag Switching and ARIS during routing transients is discussed further in Section 7.4.

Note that a topology change also affects the performance of data-driven schemes. In general, if the path of a flow changes, then for new LSRs on the path it is as if a new flow has been created. Any such flow must be forwarded conventionally at first. Thus, a topology change might place a very high burden on an LSR that has just become the new next hop for some other LSR. First, it suddenly receives a large number of flows that used to travel over some other path. Also, the normal process of new flow arrival due to new applications being started does not go away at this time. All of these flows need to be forwarded and analyzed by the flow detection algorithms. The same can happen in IP Switches if an upstream topology change causes a change of TTL for the packets in a flow. During such transients, the forwarding capacity of an IP Switch could approach the capacity of its control processor—potentially an order of magnitude less than its best case performance.

A significant performance issue for control-driven schemes arises in situations where aggregation of routes occurs. As is so often the case, we find a conflict between scalability and performance.

Figure 7.1 illustrates a situation where routing aggregation may occur. LSR X is able to reach network prefix 10.0.1/24 (the /24 means that this prefix is 24 bits long) via LSR Y, and network prefix 10.0.0/24 via LSR Z. These prefixes have the same high order 23 bits and thus can be aggregated as 10.0.0/23. Consequently, LSR X can advertise the single, aggregated prefix to LSR M. This means that, if LSRs X and M are binding labels to prefixes in their routing tables, X should only advertise a single label to LSR M for the aggregated prefix. When LSR X receives packets from LSR M that contain this label, it is not possible for LSR X to completely determine the correct forwarding for such packets from the label. Thus, LSR X would need to perform some amount of conventional forwarding using the layer 3 header. Note that LSR X may still be able to label switch many packets, for example, those going from LSR Y to LSR Z and vice versa.

This situation is the most non-ideal for control-driven LSRs. Scalability dictates that aggregation of addresses is a good thing, but at the same time aggregation creates situations where conventional forwarding must be performed rather than label switching. The effect on performance of course depends on what fraction of traffic cannot be label switched and on the relative performance of the label switching forwarding path and the conventional layer 3 forwarding path.

It should be noted that address aggregation does not happen by accident; it is deliberately chosen by network designers to improve network scalability. Thus, it is possible to predict where it will have an effect, and even to design the network such that the places where most aggregation happens are not the places where label switching is most needed, such as in the core of a high speed backbone network. Still, a network designer needs to take some care to make sure that if an LSR is placed at an aggregation point, it has enough layer 3 processing capability to handle the fraction of traffic that cannot be label switched.

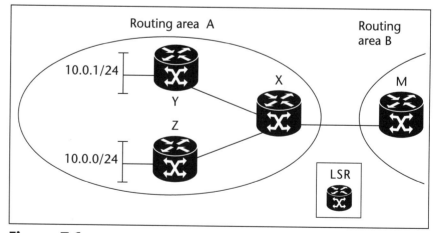

Figure 7.1   *Effect of route aggregation.*

Observe that today's data-driven schemes do not suffer any problems at aggregation points because all defined flow types are host-to-host (or finer). However, the use of more coarse-grained flow types (such as network-to-network), which is theoretically possible, would cause aggregation to become an issue for data-driven schemes as well.

7.2.2 *Scalability*

As we have already seen, performance and scalability are closely related and are often in conflict with each other. One way to assess the scaling properties of a label switching scheme is to consider how many labels need to be assigned in various scenarios.

As with performance, it is hard to get good data that enables the scalability of data-driven schemes to be determined. In general, steps to improve performance, such as increasing the sensitivity of the flow detection algorithm, have a negative impact on scalability by increasing the total number of labels that are required at any given time.

To provide a feel for the relationship between performance and scalability of data-driven approaches, we will examine some traffic data collected in September 1995, at an Internet exchange point in the San Francisco Bay Area. This data was analyzed by some researchers at Ipsilon to produce the graphs shown in Figures 7.2 and 7.3. We note that the total volume of traffic flowing through the point of collection was rather small—on the order of 30–40 Mbps—so the relevant information here is more in the trends than in the absolute numbers.

Figure 7.2 shows both the number of instantaneous connections and the number of connection setups per second required as a function of the number of packets in a flow examined before establishing a label switched path. It is clear that decreasing the flow detection sensitivity quickly reduces the total number of labels (connections) that are needed.

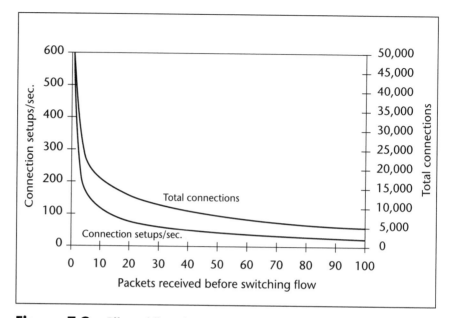

Figure 7.2   *Effect of flow detection sensitivity on label requirements.*

Figure 7.3 shows the percentage of bytes and packets that end up being label switched, again as a function of the number of packets examined at the start of each flow before it is label switched. The good news here is that the amount of data that can be switched, measured either in bytes or packets, drops much more slowly than the number of connections (labels) required as flow detection sensitivity is decreased. This means that there is a net benefit in examining more packets before deciding to label switch a flow—within limits, of course. Note that the main benefit is in setting the number of packets examined to about 10, getting us to the "knee" of the connections curve while only reducing the percentage of bytes switched by about 10%. Note also that in this case, the total number of connections (i.e., labels) needed (on the particular day that this trace was collected at one particular place) was about 15,000. The problem is in extrapolating from the available trace data to other places in the Internet on other days, or other times of day. Other points in the Internet have much larger traffic volumes and may also carry a different mixture of flows. We return to this issue in the next section. However, just the shape of the curves is encouraging, because it means that there is some hope of tuning the system to provide a good trade-off between number of connections and percentage of label switched traffic. Such tuning will obviously be much easier if traffic patterns do not change very often.

With control-driven schemes, the scaling properties depend not on the nature of the data traffic but on the properties of the control traffic, which in turn depend on factors such as the topology and design of the network. For example, in a control-driven scheme that binds a label to each prefix in the routing table, the number of labels is easy to calculate. At the time of writing, the largest routing tables—those in the Internet backbone—contain about 45,000 address prefixes. Of course, there is no necessity to bind one label to every entry in the routing table. As we saw in Section 5.1.2, for example, an LSR at the core of the Internet could bind one label to each border router of the domain it is in—on the order of a few hundred labels. Such flexibility gives control-driven approaches an edge in terms of scalability.

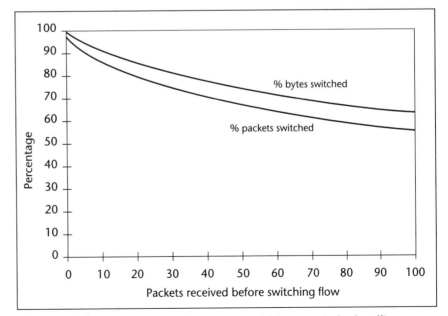

Figure 7.3   *Effect of flow detection sensitivity on switched traffic.*

7.2.3 *Robustness*

In comparing the robustness of the different approaches, we are trying to address the question "How sensitive is the performance or scalability of each scheme to changes in the network environment?" As some of the discussion in the previous sections has indicated, data-driven schemes do not seem to rate as well as control-driven schemes in this regard. The reason for this is rather intuitive: changes in the flow of data are much harder to predict than changes in the flow of control information. All that is needed to make a big change in the flow of data is a new application or a change in the usage pattern of an existing application. For example, suppose a new Website that provides some sort of transaction service such as stock quotes is attached to the Internet. Suddenly the traffic flowing to that site will consist of many short flows that cannot be flow switched, so that what might have been a small increase in total traffic could represent a large increase in load on the control processor, perhaps driving it beyond the point where it has enough bandwidth to cope.

It is not hard to think of many different scenarios where changes in user behavior or application characteristics could have a serious impact on a data-driven scheme. By contrast, it is hard to imagine the sort of change that would be required to cause a surprising degradation in the performance of a control-based scheme. For example, an Internet service provider is unlikely to find that the rate of change of routing information has become radically different over a short period of time. (If such a dramatic change did happen, it would most likely be a sign of some sort of error condition, and it would have bad effects whether or not label switching was used.) Only a truly radical change in the way networks are built, such as widespread deployment of mobile networking nodes, could cause a major surprise for a control-driven scheme.

One way to understand this major difference between data-driven and control-driven schemes is to think about data-driven schemes as a form of caching. A new flow represents a cache miss; once it has been identified as worthy of label switching, and the label switched path is established, all subsequent packets in the flow generate cache hits. In processor design, caching can provide significant performance gains if the usage pattern matches that expected by the designer. However, in the worst case, the performance of the system degrades to the performance it would have had without the cache. The challenge of designing a good caching system for the Internet is that the usage pattern is so dynamic that it almost defies characterization, and a system designed to perform well today offers no guarantees of adequate performance in the future.

7.2.4 *Soft and Hard State*

As noted in Table 7.1, the two data-driven approaches use soft state, as does ARIS, whereas Tag Switching uses a mixture of hard and soft state, depending on the type of FEC to which labels are being bound. The definitions of these terms generate a certain amount of controversy (as does the debate about the merits of each), but a reasonable working definition for our purposes is as follows:

- Soft state will time out unless refreshed periodically and thus does not require (but may use) an explicit teardown (removal) mechanism.

- Hard state will stay in place at least as long as the device storing the state stays up, unless it is explicitly torn down.

We will discuss the use of hard state by Tag Switching in Section 7.4.3. For now, we note that both data-driven approaches made the same design choice. This seems eminently sensible when one considers the difficulty of deciding exactly what a flow is and, especially, when it has ended. One might consider a flow to have finished when one has not seen any packets matching the flow identifier for some period of time, such as a minute. Of course, the flow might not really have ended at this point, but the consequences of guessing wrong are not very serious; when the next packet shows up, it is treated as the first packet of a new flow. In any case, there does not seem to be much point in having the LSR that created the label binding for a flow tell its neighbors to remove that binding when it is not even sure that the flow is finished. Better to let them time it out using whatever cache replacement strategy suits their local needs.

Thus, soft state seems like a natural choice for data-driven schemes. It provides various nice side effects. For example, in the event of a routing change causing a flow to take a different path, the no-longer-needed bindings for that flow will naturally time out, and new ones can be created along the new path without any LSR taking any special action other than updating the next hops in their routing tables.

7.2.5 *Host Support*

The penultimate row of Table 7.1 indicates that only IP Switching supports directly attached hosts under a wide range of conditions. That is, label switched paths can extend all the way to hosts rather than terminate on a label edge router. To some extent this is because the designers of IP Switching chose to provide that feature, whereas the designers of the other approaches did not, but it is also easier to provide host support in a data-driven scheme than in a control-driven scheme.

The reason for this difference is that flows, the basic entity to which labels are bound in data-driven schemes, are easily intelligible to hosts. It is, of course, necessary to run the flow detection algorithms and label binding protocol (IFMP) on the host. By contrast, most hosts do not participate in many network layer control protocols, notably routing, and thus it is harder to get them to participate in label binding when labels are bound to routes. Note that ARIS and Tag Switching can establish label switched paths all the way to hosts when RSVP is used, for the simple reason that RSVP is a control protocol in which hosts participate.

It is possible to imagine schemes by which labels that are bound to routes could be distributed to hosts that do not participate in routing, but no such scheme has been specified at the time of writing. It is also possible to run routing protocols on a host, which would then be able to bind labels just like any other LSR. However, this is a level of overhead that is generally not desirable.

One question to consider is how important it is to provide this functionality. For example, much of the same functionality could be provided by interconnecting hosts with Ethernet switches. It is mainly ATM-attached hosts that benefit from label switching all the way to the host, and these are relatively rare. In the future, it may also be useful to use label switching to end systems in environments where large numbers of hosts access a service provider network using new high speed access technologies such as Digital Subscriber Loop (DSL).

7.3 Data-Driven Approaches

Looking back at Table 7.1, we can see relatively few differences between IP Switching and the CSR approach. It should be clear from the descriptions of Chapters 3 and 4 that there is a wealth of difference in the details but that there are very few fundamental differences. It is probably fair to say that most differences can be traced to the fact that IP Switching is a real product that has been deployed, whereas CSR is more of a research effort. Thus, IP Switching has had to address real world issues such as the need to handle TTL properly and prevent loops.

One of the more significant differences between the two schemes is the attitude to ATM switched virtual circuits (SVCs). From the beginning, the CSR designers assumed that CSRs would have to be interconnected by standard ATM SVCs to be able to communicate across public ATM networks. Ipsilon, by contrast, has argued that the best thing is just to do away with ATM signalling and thus has not attempted to solve the problem of interworking with ATM SVCs. There is no reason such a capability could not be added to IP Switching or to the control-driven schemes if required.

Another significant detail is the different fields included in a flow identifier in the two approaches. The fact that IP Switching includes the TTL enables correct TTL processing and prevents the establishment of looping switched paths. Also, because IP Switching removes many fields from the header before transmitting a packet on a label switched path, it both improves the efficiency of link utilization and enables some protection against certain types of spoofing attack.

7.4 Control-Driven Approaches

The two main control-driven schemes, ARIS and Tag Switching, have much in common, but the differences in detail are quite significant. As we will see in the next chapter, resolving these differences is likely to be a major part of the IETF standardization effort for label switching. In this section we present the main differences and consider their impact.

7.4.1 Loop Prevention and Mitigation

The issue of looping is without doubt one of the areas where Tag Switching and ARIS differ most significantly. This difference can be traced in part to the different role ATM has played in the two approaches. Recall that it is the lack of a TTL field in ATM cells that makes looping such a significant issue for label switches. Tag Switching treats ATM as something of a special case and provides mechanisms to mitigate the effect of loops in that environment. By contrast, ARIS treats ATM as the normal case and thus makes loop prevention a central part of the architecture.

First, let's review the two approaches. In the non-ATM case, Tag Switching provides exactly the same degree of protection from loops that IP provides. Looping paths may be set up, but the TTL field in the tag header causes packets to be discarded if they are stuck in a loop. ARIS actually prevents the establishment of looping paths in the first place, by carrying a list of LSRs in the message that establishes the path. If an LSR sees its own identifier in this list, it knows that the ESTABLISH message has followed a loop, and thus it aborts the attempt to create a label switched path.

In the ATM case, nothing changes for ARIS. For Tag Switching, the method of establishing label bindings changes to downstream on demand, and the use of hop count fields in the binding requests and responses prevents the establishment of a stable looping path. However, because the hop count field must reach its maximum allowed value, this may take longer than the ARIS approach. This is similar to the "count to infinity" problem found in some routing protocols.

The ARIS approach is very conservative with regard to loops. If there is any chance of a loop, the switched path is torn down. This means that any routing change in a network of ARIS ISRs will cause existing switched paths to be torn down and replaced. This may happen even if no loops were present at any time.

Consider the example network in Figure 7.4. Assume that, at some point in time, the shortest path from LSR D to LSR A is via LSR B. Then, at some later time, the shortest path from LSR D to A changes so that it is now via LSR C. In the ARIS scheme, when LSR D detects this change, it must stop forwarding packets toward A on the label switched path and send a TRIGGER message to LSR C. It is not allowed to "remember" an old ESTABLISH message that it might have received from C in the past, because routing has changed since that message was sent. While D waits for an ESTAB-LISH message to come back from C (and until D verifies that the path provided by C is loop-free), it must do one of two things with packets destined for A: drop them, or forward them using longest match in its control processor.

Note that this happens even though there was never a looping path. There would have been no negative consequence of forwarding packets toward B until the new binding was received from C. The negative effects of dropping packets are fairly clear. The consequences of taking the other option—forwarding the packets in the control processor—are more serious than might be appreciated at first. A closer look will explain why.

We have seen that an LSR has a control component and a label switching component and that the label switching path could be implemented in a variety of ways (e.g., using the hardware of an ATM switch). When a packet cannot be forwarded by the label switching component, it is forwarded by the control component using conventional longest match forwarding. In many cases we find that the forwarding performance of the control component is significantly less than that of the label switching path. If this were not true, then why not forward all packets in the control processor? Thus, diverting a large amount of traffic to be forwarded by the control component during routing transients is likely to overwhelm the control processor. Of course, this is exactly the wrong thing to do, since the main thing that the control processor needs to do at this time is to focus on routing updates and the reconvergence of routing. Dropping packets in this case is probably the lesser of two evils.

As an aside, we note that the above argument is not strictly limited to label switching routers. Many conventional routers have a "fast path" for the common case and a "slow path" for uncommon cases. If a situation arises where all packets follow the slow path during periods of routing instability, the performance can be disastrously bad. Designers of modern routers generally try to avoid such failure modes.

The basic problem with a conservative approach to loop avoidance is this: it is virtually impossible to avoid loops completely without sometimes taking unnecessary steps, like discarding packets that were on nonlooping paths. It is difficult to predict how frequently this will happen, because it depends greatly on the network environment.

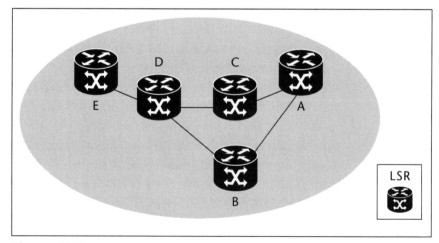

Figure 7.1   *Effect of routing change on ARIS and Tag Switched paths.*

It is important to realize that, in the absence of misconfiguration, loops are a transient phenomenon. They are also a fact of life with connectionless routing protocols. Tag Switching accepts that they happen and tries to ensure that the consequences are not too severe, just as conventional IP does. ARIS tries to avoid them at all costs, with the result that some packet loss during routing transients—even those that caused no looping—is inevitable.

7.4.2 *Ordered Versus Independent Binding*

Closely related to the preceding discussion is another significant difference between ARIS and Tag Switching. Label bindings in ARIS are ordered, in the sense that they propagate in an orderly fashion from the egress of a region of ISRs toward the ingress. Each non-egress ISR must receive an ESTABLISH message from its downstream neighbor before propagating the binding to its upstream neighbors. For Tag Switching, in the common case of destination-based routing, bindings are independent: any Tag Switch in the network can establish label bindings and advertise them without waiting for a neighbor to instigate the process. (Note that Tag Switching, like ARIS, uses the ordered approach when establishing explicitly routed paths.)

Both ordered and independent approaches have advantages and drawbacks. The ordered approach helps to provide ARIS's loop prevention capability that was described above (which also has advantages and drawbacks). A less apparent consequence of the choice between ordered and independent approaches is that it affects the way Forwarding Equivalence Classes (FECs) are selected for label bindings. Clearly, with the independent approach, each LSR makes its own choice about how it will partition the set of possible packets into FECs. For example, it might decide that each prefix in its routing table will represent an FEC. If neighboring LSRs make different decisions about the FECs they will use, then it will not be possible to establish label switched paths for some of those FECs. Normally, the neighboring LSRs are configured so that this does not happen. However, this is exactly what happens when an LSR aggregates routes at an area boundary, as we discussed in Section 7.2.1.

In the ordered approach, the selection of FECs can be made at the egress LSR. As a binding (the ARIS ESTABLISH message) propagates upstream, all LSRs use the same FEC as was chosen at the egress—there is no chance of different choices being made by different LSRs. All that is required is that the LSRs are able to determine the next hop for the FEC in question, so that it can determine whether the binding came from the correct next hop.

The fact that intermediate LSRs don't have to choose the same FECs is an advantage of the ordered approach, but it can be applied only in relatively few situations, such as when setting up a label switched path that passes through a point of routing aggregation. Furthermore, this capability comes at the cost of reduced scalability—the result is setting up more labels than prefixes in the routing tables of those LSRs using the aggregated routes. Thus, the scaling advantages of aggregation are somewhat reduced.

The downside of the ordered approach is an increase in the amount of time that it takes to set up a label switched path. In general, the ordered approach requires that bindings propagate across an entire region of LSRs before a label switched path is established. During the period when this is going on, packets must either be dropped or processed using longest match in the control processor, neither of which is desirable. By contrast, the independent approach allows every LSR to establish and advertise label bindings at any time, without the delay of waiting for messages to propagate in order from one side of the network to the other. Furthermore, the fact that Tag Switches can remember label bindings from neighbors who were not next hops at the time of advertisement enables almost instantaneous establishment of new label switched paths when routing changes.

It can be argued that, because each approach has advantages, allowing one or the other to be used in different situations would be ideal. In fact, just such a compromise has been adopted by the MPLS working group.

7.4.3 *Label Distribution Protocol Issues*

The label distribution protocol for the ARIS scheme is called simply the ARIS protocol, whereas Tag Switching uses a protocol known as TDP (Tag Distribution Protocol). As one might expect, there are plenty of similarities, since both are doing the same job of binding labels to address prefixes most of the time. However, there are some significant differences. Some of these variations arise from the differences already described between the two approaches, such as the contrasts in loop prevention and mitigation schemes. However, some of the differences, which are described below, are specifically related to the design of the protocol.

Transport Reliability

Both ARIS and TDP require reliable, in-order delivery of messages. The need for reliability is clear: If a label binding or a request for a binding is not successfully delivered, then traffic cannot be label switched and will have to be handled by the control processor or dropped. It is also easy to find examples where the order of message delivery is important: a binding advertisement followed by a withdrawal of that binding, for example, will have a very different effect if the messages are received in the reverse order.

TDP provides this reliability using TCP, the most widely used reliable transport protocol. A pair of TDP peers establish a TCP connection between themselves and then use this connection for the transmission of all messages. This makes the design of TDP itself rather simple: it can assume that any message it sends will be received correctly by the remote peer in the order it was sent.

ARIS, by contrast, runs directly over IP, and thus reliability needs to be built into the ARIS protocol itself. Thus we see ACKNOWLEDGE messages as part of the ARIS protocol, for example. The idea is to provide exactly the level of functionality needed and no more. For example, TCP provides a congestion avoidance mechanism that may not be strictly necessary for a neighbor-to-neighbor control protocol, and the complete ordering of messages that it provides is more strict than required for label distribution.

The advantages of building reliability into the label distribution protocol, however, may well be outweighed by the drawbacks. For

example, because every ESTABLISH message must be acknowl-
edged, there needs to be a timer for every unacknowledged message. By contrast, TDP delegates the timer function to TCP, which
can use a single timer for the whole session. The overhead of man-
aging large numbers of timers can be significant.

TCP provides a wealth of useful functions that TDP is able to
use for free, such as efficient packing of higher layer messages into
IP packets, piggybacking of ACKs on data packets, and flow control.
Unlike congestion control, flow control (making sure that a
sender does not overrun the capacity of a receiver) is necessary for
a control protocol.

Transport protocol design is notoriously difficult, and there have
been plenty of efforts to "improve" on TCP that have ultimately
failed to do so. There are many details to get right and special cases
to consider, such as ensuring that old messages from closed sessions
are not accepted erroneously by new sessions. This argues in favor
of using a well-tested protocol rather than reinventing the wheel.

Piggybacking on Other Protocols

TDP and the ARIS protocol play slightly different roles in their
respective architectures. TDP is designed as the protocol to be used
when no other, more appropriate protocol is available. Thus, for
example, BGP, PIM, and RSVP may all be used to distribute label
bindings. TDP is used for distributing label bindings in the case of
destination-based routing only. By contrast, ARIS is used for label
binding distribution in all cases except one: RSVP.

The consequence of piggybacking, as it is done in the Tag
Switching architecture, is that label binding distribution is more
easily synchronized with the control traffic that caused labels to
be allocated in the first place. The functionality required of the
new protocol is also reduced. The downside of this approach is
that more protocols have to be modified to achieve the desired
functionality. One also has to be concerned about the possibility
that a label, piggybacked in a protocol message, might be received
by a device that does not understand labels. Either this must be
prevented or the piggybacking must be done in a way that non–
label switching devices are easily able to ignore label bindings
received in this way.

Hard or Soft State

Whereas the data-driven approaches unquestionably use soft state, Tag Switching and ARIS are a little harder to classify. In the cases where Tag Switching piggybacks label distribution on top of an existing protocol such as PIM, RSVP, or BGP, it inherits the hard or soft state of the protocol. BGP uses hard state; PIM and RSVP use soft. Similarly, when ARIS uses RSVP for label distribution, the result is a soft state approach.

For cases where TDP is used, Tag Switching is a hard state approach. The reason for this is primarily efficiency. Because TDP runs over a reliable transport, it can be assumed that all messages sent to peers will eventually be received correctly. Thus there is never a need to refresh the state of a peer. All that is ever needed is to make incremental changes: adding new label bindings and withdrawing old ones as required. Thus, when routing is stable, there is no TDP traffic between peers, except for periodic KEEP-ALIVE messages that let a TSR know that its peers are still alive and connected. If the KEEPALIVE does not arrive, the TDP peer is assumed to be down and all labels learned from it are deleted.

In general, Tag Switching tries to use the same type of state that the underlying control information uses. This happens naturally in the cases where labels are piggybacked on other protocols, but we might wonder how close the match is when TDP is used. In this case, the underlying control information is unicast routing. In fact, routing information is difficult to classify as hard or soft state. However, we observe that OSPF, a very common routing protocol, and TDP are quite similar in their state distribution. Although OSPF does occasionally refresh routing information (on the order of every few hours), it mostly just sends KEEPALIVE messages to keep the state installed, just like TDP. It also uses explicit acknowledgments to ensure that the data arrived, rather than resending it periodically. In this way, TDP and OSPF show considerable similarity in the "hardness" of their state information.

We mentioned in Section 7.2.4 that soft state was a natural fit for data-driven approaches because of the difficulty of deciding when to delete a binding for a flow. The converse argument can be applied to control-driven schemes. It is easy for an LSR to determine that it has gained or lost an entry in its routing table, for example, and that it therefore needs to modify the set of label bindings that it advertises to its peers. Thus it is easy to explicitly delete state that is no longer needed and to advertise only changes to old state without constantly refreshing it.

Interestingly, the ARIS protocol does use soft state. Even though hard state could be used, the protocol requires that label bindings are refreshed within some time interval or else they will time out. This is a conservative design choice that backs up the reliable message delivery with periodic refreshes. The cost of the extra level of reliability is complexity: the refresh mechanism requires the maintenance of a set of timers for all label bindings so that the advertiser of bindings knows when to re-advertise them to prevent time out. As with the timers used for reliability, this may increase the overhead in an implementation of the protocol.

7.4.4 *Support for Hierarchy*

Both Tag Switching and ARIS provide support for nested label switched paths. However, the procedures by which such paths are established in these two proposals are significantly different. The following discussion outlines some of the major differences.

Consider packets flowing from left to right in Figure 7.5. There are four label switched paths: (X, A, B, C, Y), (X, A, B, C, V), (W, A, B, C, Y), and (W, A, B, C, V). These paths are nested into another label switched path: (A, B, C).

With Tag Switching, LSR B has no information about Y or V. This is because Tag Switching allows A and C to exchange label bindings directly (e.g., using BGP). With ARIS, even though LSR B need not maintain any forwarding state for Y or V, B is required to keep egress identifiers and labels for Y and V (this information is contained in the Tunnel Object carried by the ESTABLISH message that B receives from C). So, while both Tag Switching and ARIS approaches result in reducing the amount of forwarding state in B, only Tag Switching also reduces the amount of label binding information that has to be maintained by an LSR. Thus the Tag Switching approach results in better scalability than ARIS.

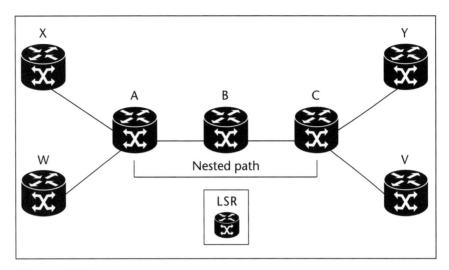

Figure 7.5 *Hierarchical network example.*

With Tag Switching, A obtains label binding information for Y and V directly from C, without any involvement of B. This, in turn, implies that A and C need to have a mechanism to exchange this information directly with each other. Suitable mechanisms include BGP and TDP. With ARIS, on the other hand, A obtains this information from B. Thus, A and C do not exchange label binding information directly.

With ARIS, any changes to the label switched path outside of a tunnel would require all the LSRs along the tunnel to be informed of such changes. In contrast, with Tag Switching, none of the LSRs along the tunnel (except for the ingress LSR) need to be aware of such changes. This results in greater stability for the Tag Switching approach than for ARIS.

Tag Switching defines procedures and encapsulations to support arbitrary levels of nesting. In contrast, the ARIS specifications allow for up to two levels of nesting. However, at the time of writing, the ARIS specifications lack some of the required detail on the procedures and encapsulations for multiple levels of nesting.

7.4.5 *Encapsulations*

As we have seen in the two previous chapters, ARIS and Tag Switching each have a proposed method for carrying labels on media other than ATM. In these cases there is more flexibility because we are not constrained to put labels in the VCI/VPI field to leverage the capabilities of ATM switch hardware. The major differences between the two approaches are

- The Tag Switching encapsulation applies to both LAN media and point-to-point links, whereas the ARIS proposal is for LANs only.

- The Tag Switching encapsulation includes a TTL field; ARIS does not.

- The ARIS proposal puts the label inside the MAC header, whereas Tag Switching puts it between the MAC header and the layer 3 header.

There are some advantages and disadvantages to each approach. Fitting the label into the MAC header means that a packet does not get any longer when it has a label applied to it. Thus, if a host had sent a packet that equaled the link maximum transmission unit (MTU), it would not exceed the MTU after label imposition. However, this scenario is best avoided by using path MTU discovery, which is recommended behavior for hosts and becoming widely deployed.

Although putting the label in the MAC header might seem logical by analogy to the placement of labels in the ATM header, the analogy does not hold up. Devices that forward based on the MAC header—bridges and LAN switches, for example—are not generally capable of label swapping, so there is not much advantage to putting the label where they can find it. Also, the idea of "stealing" a field that has a particular meaning and giving it another is likely to cause problems when deploying such an approach. For example, an environment where some conventional bridges are running alongside LSRs using an encapsulation that puts labels in the address fields of the MAC header can behave in undesirable ways, leading to packet duplication and possible looping. It is also possible that bridge tables will overflow because of the increase in the number of "MAC addresses" they need to store.

The fact that labels are carried in the MAC address field in the ARIS scheme creates considerable problems for routers and hosts. They are effectively forced to operate in promiscuous mode, which will have a serious performance impact.

The lack of a TTL in the ARIS encapsulation is justified by the fact that there is no TTL in the ATM encapsulation either, and the same loop prevention and TTL adjustment techniques can be used in both cases. Because these techniques have disadvantages discussed above, dispensing with them by adding a TTL field, and thus providing equivalent loop mitigation behavior to conventional IP, seems appealing.

7.5 Label Switching or Conventional Routing?

This entire book has been devoted to the subject of label switching, and we have generally avoided discussion of the design of routers that are not based on label switching. However, when we discussed the motivations behind the invention of the various label switching approaches, we observed that much of the motivation came from perceived shortcomings of conventional routers. Thus it seems appropriate at this stage to revisit conventional routers briefly and to compare them with the label switching schemes. In particular, the field of router design has been far from dormant while label switching has been developing, so we need to ask whether label switching addresses a real need or not. In this discussion, it is important to define what a "conventional" router is. We defined it as a device that forwards IP packets by a full examination of the IP header, rather than using a label to make the forwarding decision. Thus, many new devices with high speed interfaces and multigigabit throughputs may fall into the category of conventional routers.

One of the most easily understood claims made for label switching is that it improves performance and does so at lower cost than conventional approaches. Because there are now conventional routers on the market with comparable performance to ATM switches (e.g., 10 ports of OC-12, or 6 Gbps of total bandwidth) the performance claim can be called into question. Some recent advances in algorithms to implement the longest match algorithm also suggest that very high speed longest match implementation is possible. The cost angle is harder to figure out, because vendor list prices are not necessarily a good indication of the real cost of a device. Cost is driven by a mixture of technical and economic factors, and the latter are largely beyond the scope of this book. However, there are a few observations we can make about cost.

First, we should observe that label switching only reduces the cost of the header lookup and forwarding decision. Even if this could be driven to zero (clearly the best case, albeit an unlikely one), the impact on the cost of the whole system remains modest. The reason is that there are many other costs in building a device that can forward packets at many gigabits per second, such as the cost of the switching fabric itself and, very importantly, the cost of buffering. Buffering can be a large part of the cost of a high performance router, because high speed links increase both the required speed of the buffer memory and the total buffering requirements for good application performance.[2]

Thus, there are limits to how much cost label switching can save, as a percentage of the total cost of a router. However, a slightly more subtle claim about cost has been made by Ipsilon, and it is applicable to all label switching routers, since all can be made using the same hardware components. This claim is that ATM switches are becoming "commodity" items in much the same way that PCs are. With lots of vendors making ATM switches with near identical functionality (a situation that does not pertain to routers today), we might expect the *price* (as opposed to parts

---

[2] The reasoning behind this depends on the fact that TCP performs best when the routers in the path can buffer roughly bandwidth times round-triptime of data. Increased bandwidth means increased buffer needs.

cost) of these devices to drop because of competition. Furthermore, if enough ATM switches are made using common chip technology, the cost of chipsets needed for ATM switches might also drop, just as PC chipsets have done. Thus, there seems to be a possible cost advantage for label switching routers that can be made from two commodity devices: an ATM switch and a PC. Whether this theory turns out to be true is something that only time will tell.

Our conclusion is that arguments about price and performance in the label switching versus conventional routing debate are inconclusive. Certainly the potential exists for label switching to reduce cost at a certain performance level, but it is yet to be clearly demonstrated. Such arguments may ultimately have more to do with economics than technology. Furthermore, they miss the most important issues. These issues are the improvements in functionality, scalability, evolvability, and integration that label switching brings.

7.5.1 *Functionality*

Label switching enables various pieces of new functionality that were either unavailable or inefficient with conventional routing. A good example of this is explicit route support. Because the decision to send a packet down an explicit route is made only at the beginning of the explicitly routed path, explicit route support is more efficient than prior schemes, such as the source route option in IP. Also, policies that could not be implemented in IP (e.g., because they depend on information that is only available to the router at the start of the explicit path) can be implemented using label switching.

7.5.2 *Scalability*

We saw in Section 5.1.2 how the scalability of routing could be improved with label switching by providing more complete separation between interdomain and intradomain routing. This separation also leads to more stable interior routing.

7.5.3 *IP/ATM Integration*

Label switching makes it easier to transmit IP data over networks of ATM switches, removing the need for many complex procedures and protocols to deal with issues such as address resolution and the different models of multicast and resource reservation. Improving the integration of IP and ATM is particularly worthwhile in networks where ATM is used for a variety of functions (such as carrying voice or frame relay traffic) as well as supporting IP. Although we might be able to imagine a world in which everything runs over IP and integration with ATM is not important, that is definitely not the world of today. Investment in ATM as a core technology is sufficiently advanced in many places that integration of IP and ATM is vitally important.

7.5.4 *Evolvability*

Because label switching cleanly separates the control and forwarding functions, it becomes easier to evolve the control functionality. Adding some new piece of routing functionality, for example, requires no change to the forwarding mechanism. This contrasts with the conventional model, where adding new functions such as multicast and resource reservation significantly alters the forwarding path.

7.6 Label Switching Versus MPOA

As we mentioned in Chapter 1, all the label switching approaches described in this book were motivated to various degrees by the desire to facilitate integration of ATM and IP. The ATM Forum efforts in this area resulted in the development of Multiprotocol over ATM (MPOA). Thus it seems appropriate to compare MPOA with label switching.

The first thing to observe is that MPOA and label switching each solve a somewhat different set of problems but that the sets partially overlap. For example, MPOA solves problems of communication among bridges on a single ATM subnet, which is not something that label switching addresses. Similarly, MPOA does not solve the problem of multicast communication among routers connected to a single ATM network in different subnets, which label switching does address. The area where the problem spaces most closely overlap is in establishing unicast communication among routers connected to an ATM network. A simple example of this is shown in Figure 7.6. Recall that in the classical IP model, routers A and E would not be able to communicate directly across the ATM cloud but would communicate via router C. MPOA enables a shortcut to be established between router A and router E that passes through the two ATM switches, bypassing router C. Similarly, any of the label switching approaches described in this book enable router A to communicate with router E over a label switched path through the two switches, provided those switches are able to function as LSRs (i.e., provided that they run IP control protocols and a label binding protocol).

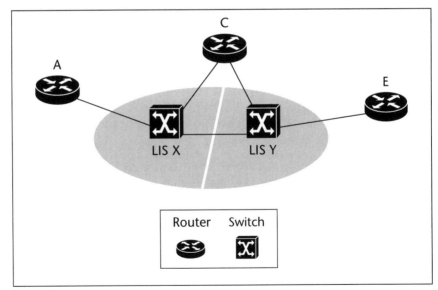

Figure 7.6   *MPOA and label switching example.*

In setting up intersubnet shortcuts, MPOA uses the Next Hop Resolution Protocol (NHRP). One of the most significant drawbacks with NHRP is that, when run between routers, it can introduce *persistent* forwarding loops. The environments in which NHRP can be applied must be constrained to prevent this from happening. NHRP also requires a number of servers to enable the originator of the shortcut to determine the ATM address of the egress router, which it can then use to signal for a VC. Thus, there is a reasonable degree of complexity to set up the shortcut compared to establishing a label switched path. And the fact that NHRP is limited to unicast traffic further circumscribes its applicability.

Most of the other problems solved by MPOA are problems that label switching does not address. We have already mentioned bridging across a single ATM subnet. This seems worthwhile—to support non-IP or non-routable protocols, for example. However, this functionality can also be provided simply by using LAN emulation (LANE).

One notable problem addressed by MPOA is the replacement of a device that acts as both a bridge and a router with an MPOA-capable bridge. It is less clear whether this problem is worth solving. One common claim is that a combination of a bridge and a router is more expensive and harder to manage than an MPOA-capable bridge. So far there is no conclusive evidence to support this claim. It is clear that an MPOA-capable bridge is a more complex device than a conventional bridge. At the same time, it is not that clear whether an MPOA-capable bridge is significantly simpler than a device that combines a bridge and a router.

In summary, MPOA and label switching mostly address different problems. Where there is overlap, label switching seems the simpler and more generally applicable solution.

7.7 Summary

All label switching approaches have certain characteristics in common, such as the ability to run on standard ATM hardware and the use of IP routing protocols to determine routing. They all use some sort of new protocol to distribute bindings between labels and FECs. However, there are many significant differences, some of which are fundamental to the respective architectures, some of which just reflect the priorities of the design teams in picking features to address. The most important difference between schemes is the choice between a data-driven or control-driven approach.

The biggest drawback to a data-driven approach seems to be the difficulty in predicting performance because it depends so much on the detailed characteristics of the offered traffic. A small change in the length or number of flows passing through a point may cause a large change in the percentage of traffic that can be switched, resulting in overload of the control processor.

Ipsilon's IP Switching and Toshiba's CSR are data-driven approaches. They rely on the identification of a flow and some heuristics to decide when to assign a label to a flow. They bear some resemblance to caching algorithms. Both use a soft state model for label binding distribution. IP Switching has a number of features absent from CSR, such as TTL handling and loop prevention. The most notable feature provided by CSR not found in the other schemes is a way to interoperate with standard ATM SVCs, using the VCID mechanism described in Chapter 3.

Tag Switching and ARIS are control-driven approaches. A key difference is in the approach to looping: ARIS prevents establishment of looping label switched paths, whereas Tag Switching uses TTL mechanisms to mitigate the effect of loops, just as conventional IP does. ARIS uses ordered label distribution; Tag Switching uses an independent approach. The result of both these choices is that there are more situations where ARIS cannot label switch packets for some period of time and must either resort to layer 3 forwarding or dropping. However, ARIS can create label switched paths through points of routing aggregation, at the cost of loss of scalability.

Tag Switching and ARIS also differ in their LAN encapsulations and in the details of their label binding distribution protocols. The notable protocol differences are the decision to build reliability into ARIS rather than run over TCP as Tag Switching's protocol does and the fact that ARIS requires refreshing of bindings, making it a soft state approach.

The other issue addressed in this chapter is whether label switching truly offers advantages over more conventional routing techniques, especially in the light of recent advances in that area. Our conclusion is that it may be hard to justify label switching from a performance or cost standpoint alone, but that label switching offers real advantages in routing functionality, scalability, and IP/ATM integration and will make it easier to develop the capabilities of routers in the future.

Further Reading

For some excellent work in the area of improving routing performance without resorting to label switching, we recommend two papers:

Brodnik, A., S. Carlsson, M. Degermark, and S. Pink. "Small Forwarding Tables for Fast Routing Lookups." In Proceedings of ACM SIGCOMM 97, Cannes, France, September 1997.

Waldvogel, M., G. Varghese, J. Turner, and B. Plattner. "Scalable High Speed IP Routing Lookups." In Proceedings of ACM SIGCOMM 97, Cannes, France, September 1997.

Many of the references given in earlier chapters are also relevant. The Tag Switching publications stress the non–performance related benefits of label switching, and some of Ipsilon's publications describe efforts to characterize the performance of IP Switching. Finally, there is at least one Website dedicated to comparing label switching approaches, which is updated as new approaches appear:

www.csl.sony.co.jp/person/demizu/inet/mlr.html

Because the behavior during routing transients and looping issues are important in the comparison of different approaches, the following paper, which provides a thorough study of such issues in the Internet, may be of interest:

Paxson, V., "End-to-End Routing Behavior in the Internet." *IEEE/ACM Transactions on Networking* 5, no. 5, October 1997, 601–15.

Chapter

8

Multiprotocol Label Switching (MPLS)

We have considered the fundamental concepts that underlie the label switching approaches, and we have looked at four of them in detail. The IETF's MPLS working group is engaged in trying to define a standard approach to label switching. In this chapter we examine this group and its endeavors in more depth.

At the time of writing, the group has met three times officially, plus its original Birds of a Feather (BOF) at the 37th IETF in December 1996. If all goes well, the group is likely to continue its work at least through the end of 1998, and probably longer. At this juncture, therefore, we are presenting a review of work in progress, albeit work that seems pointed in an easily discernible direction. This is in marked contrast to the material we have covered so far. All of the approaches we looked at earlier have been implemented and used in trials, and one, IP Switching, has been on sale for some time. At present there is no complete specification for an MPLS system, much less any implementation.

We begin with a brief survey of the working group's history and examine its charter. Having seen the task the group set itself, we consider the progress made so far. Although some good progress has been made in reconciling different approaches, several unresolved issues remain; we consider the most important of them. Finally, we also offer some predictions about the likely progress of the group in the future.

8.1 The MPLS Working Group

Before considering the current progress in the MPLS WG we establish the context by reviewing the steps that led to the group's formation, its composition, and its charter.

8.1.1 Origins and Charter

The group was formally chartered by the IETF in the spring of 1997 after the December 1996 BOF established beyond a doubt that there was sufficient interest to form a working group—an estimated 800 people attended the session, perhaps creating a record. The impetus to form the group had come from Cisco Systems, which had declared its intention to pursue standardization of label switching at the time the first Tag Switching Internet drafts were published. Support was quickly forthcoming from several other companies, notably IBM. The working group was formed with two co-chairs representing Cisco and IBM.

The charter of the MPLS working group is available on-line at the IETF Website. It is only four pages long, but it took several revisions and a considerable amount of time to reach agreement on its contents. The document contains, in addition to some administrative details, two main sections. The first, entitled "Description of Working Group," has subsections for problem statement, high level requirements, charter statement, and objectives. The second section covers goals and milestones.

8.1.2 Description of Working Group

The problem statement should look familiar to readers of this book, as it describes the problems that the approaches described in the preceding chapters have tried to solve. It mentions scalability and flexibility of network layer routing, increasing forwarding performance, and simplification of the integration of routers with cell switching technologies. As we have seen, these are all areas where solutions based on a label switching paradigm hold some promise.

The high level requirements are that the solution developed by the MPLS WG must work with existing datalink technologies and routing protocols, although it may propose "appropriate optimizations." It must allow a variety of forwarding granularities to be associated with a label, and it must address hierarchical networks and the issues of scalability.

The charter statement itself asserts that the group is responsible for standardizing a base technology for using label forwarding in conjunction with network layer routing over a variety of media. The base technology is expected to include procedures and protocols for label distribution, encapsulation, support of multicast, reservation and QoS mechanisms, and, lastly, definition of host behaviors.

The objectives subsection is essentially a to do list. The objectives require the group to specify label maintenance and distribution protocols that support unicast, multicast, a hierarchy of routing knowledge, and explicit paths. An encapsulation specification is also required (in a somewhat ambiguously worded sentence).[1] The ATM technology is called out for special treatment in a way that reflects its importance to label switching technology. A protocol to allow direct host participation is to be specified. It seems that direct host attachment to label switched networks is of low priority for the members of the working group since no contributions have been made on this subject at the time of writing. As we noted in Chapter 7, host participation in label switching is a little easier in data-driven approaches, and the MPLS group is focused on a control-driven approach. Finally, the WG is required to "discuss" the issue of QoS, which leaves open the possibility of not

---

[1] The sentence says, "Specify standard procedures of carrying label information over various link level technologies." Although this might be interpreted as referring to a label distribution protocol, it is intended to mean that label encapsulations for a variety of link technologies, of the type that are described in Chapters 5 and 6, should be developed.

actually standardizing anything in this area. Given the importance of QoS and the amount of work being devoted to it in other areas of the network community, MPLS will almost certainly have to address it in some way.

8.1.3 *Goals and Milestones*

Most of the goals and milestones of the working group follow directly from the objectives. Like most working groups, the MPLS group needs to produce a number of documents specifying protocols and procedures for using them. In addition, there is a requirement for a pair of documents: "Framework" and "Architecture." The full set of documents to be produced is listed below. The dates in parentheses are the original target dates for submission of the documents to the Internet Engineering Steering Group (IESG).

- Informational RFCs
  - ❏ Framework (March 1997)
  - ❏ Architecture (June 1997)
- Standards Track RFCs
  - ❏ Unicast Label Distribution Protocol (LDP) (August 1997)
  - ❏ Multicast LDP (October 1997)
  - ❏ Operation over ATM (December 1997)
  - ❏ Encapsulation (December 1997)
  - ❏ Host Behavior (April 1998)

At the time of writing, 10 months after the WG was chartered, the milestone dates look absurdly ambitious. With the exception of the host behavior document, all of the above were due to have been finished. The fact that none of them has does not mean, however, that there has been no progress. There have been a large number of somewhat uncoordinated contributions (Internet drafts) to the group. Many of them may find a place in the final outcome of the group's work. A smaller number of documents are being produced by small design teams at the suggestion of the area director and/or the WG's co-chairs. These include the framework and architecture documents and the specification of the LDP for unicast traffic. As of the Washington meeting of the IETF in December 1997, the framework document had reached its third revision. The architecture and LDP documents have been presented only once.

An important preliminary step to producing IETF standards is to produce Internet drafts that are the formal output of a working group rather than of individuals. At the time of writing, the MPLS working group has adopted the following drafts as working group documents:

- Framework
- Architecture
- Label Distribution Protocol
- Generic Encapsulation
- Label Distribution for RSVP Flows

As working group documents, these papers are expected to form the basis of the standards that MPLS ultimately will produce. We provide details on each in the sections that follow.

The one draft that does not require much discussion is that dealing with generic encapsulation. This draft covers encapsulation of labeled packets on non-ATM links. The encapsulation that the working group has adopted for these links is the one described in Section 5.2.1. Encapsulation on ATM links will, of course, use the VCI and/or VPI field to carry labels.

8.2 The MPLS Framework

The framework document was produced by authors from Ascend Communications, Bay Networks, Cisco, and IBM. It is an attempt to collect the sort of information that would help someone answer the question "What is this MPLS stuff all about?"—a sort of "MPLS 101." The document's authors actually envisioned it doing more than that, however. They recognized that the architecture would have to be designed drawing elements from a range of possibilities, and it was felt that for the benefit of the architecture design team and of the group as a whole the framework should include descriptions of these. There was also an awareness that the framework could serve some historical function; for approaches that didn't make it into the architecture specification there would at least be some record that they had been considered.

The framework document overlaps somewhat with the specifications that came after it and that draw in part on the insights made in it. It is probably less useful now than it was earlier in the WG's life. It is a useful introduction to the subject matter and approaches of the WG, but we hope that at this stage of this book most readers would find little in the framework that they have not already encountered here.

8.3 The MPLS Architecture

The MPLS architecture document is the work of a design team formed after the Memphis IETF meeting in April 1997. The team consisted of representatives from Cisco Systems, IBM, and Ascend Communications. Given the composition of the team (which reflects the most active players in the working group as a whole), it should come as no surprise that the emerging architecture is close to a union of the Tag Switching and ARIS proposals. A number of issues are still open; as an example the issue of egress versus local control (corresponding to the independent versus order creation of bindings discussed in Chapter 2) is sufficiently contentious that separate appendixes are provided detailing the merits of the two approaches.

The proposed architecture uses downstream assignment of labels for unicast traffic. It allows labels to be globally unique, unique per node, or unique per interface. Labels are allowed to have a variety of granularities; the document acknowledges the problems that arise when there is a mismatch of granularity between neighboring LSRs. A last in first out (LIFO) label stack, such as the one specified for Tag Switching, is employed as the mechanism for supporting hierarchical labels. Forwarding decisions are always made on the label at the top of the stack.

Two alternative path selection mechanisms are proposed for the architecture: hop by hop and explicit routing. With the hop by hop mechanism, the next hop is chosen using the results of the normal network layer routing computations. An explicit route is completely specified by the source. All LSRs are required to be able to forward explicitly routed packets, but they do not have to be capable of originating them.

The topology-driven nature of label assignment is, perhaps somewhat surprisingly, not stated explicitly in the document (although it was clearly stated when the architecture was presented at the August 1997 IETF meeting). The architecture does not define an encapsulation for labeled data, but does allow for two options: using an encapsulation specifically developed for MPLS, or using "available locations" in the datalink or network layer encapsulations. (The ATM VCI/VPI fields are the obvious example of this.) Although the generic MPLS encapsulation is not defined here, the necessary components are: the label stack, a TTL field, and a Class of Service field.

The requirement for TTL processing that appears later in the document is interesting and has been the source of some discord on the MPLS mailing list. The architecture proposes that the TTL should have the same value at the end of a label switched path (or hierarchy of them) as it would have had if it had traversed the same sequence of LSRs without being label switched. Note that this is subtly different from requiring that the TTL be processed in the same way as it is in conventional routers. A compromise is clearly necessary if existing ATM switch hardware is to be used for MPLS.

A large section of the architecture document deals with the special case of ATM. The various possible encodings of labels in the VCI and VPI fields are discussed, as are the scaling problems that have led to the notion of VC-merge and VC-merge capable hardware.

In addition to defining the basic technology and much new terminology, the architecture provides a whole section detailing possible uses of MPLS. These include application to normally and explicitly routed traffic, to tunneling, to multicast (which is discussed only briefly), and in backbone networks to support tunneling between BGP peers.

There remain a number of issues on which the team that produced this document is yet to agree, the most significant of which we consider in Section 8.5. Before doing so, it is worth listing the characteristics of the architecture on which there is consensus:

- Topology/control-driven label binding
- Downstream label assignment
- Variable label granularity
- LIFO label stack
- Support for hierarchy
- Provision of TTL "fixup"
- Encapsulation to include TTL and QoS
- (Some of the) specifics of usage over ATM

8.4 The Label Distribution Protocol (LDP)

The initial LDP specification is the work of a design team that includes authors from Cisco, Bay Networks, Ericsson, and IBM and that was formed after the 39th IETF meeting, in Munich. We have seen that the architecture is based on a control-driven model; as a consequence the proposal for an LDP is based on a union of the (control-driven) TDP and ARIS protocols.

The design team deliberately restricted itself to a relatively small solution space for the first draft of the protocol, which included

- Unicast and multicast label distribution
- Explicit routing
- Allowing egress and local control

In fact, at the 40th IETF meeting, not even all these topics had been fully specified. The draft specified a protocol that has the following basic characteristics:

- It provides an LSR "discovery" mechanism to enable LSR peers to establish communication.
- It runs over TCP to provide reliable delivery of messages.
- It defines two classes of messages:
  - Adjacency messages, which deal with initialization, kee-palive, and shutdown
  - Label Advertisement messages, which deal with label binding advertisements, requests, withdrawal, and release
- It is designed to be easily extensible, using messages specified as collections of TLV encoded objects.

The TLV (type, length, value) encoding means that each object contains a type field to say what sort of object it is (e.g., a label binding), a length field to say how long the object is, and a value field, the meaning of which depends on the type. New capabilities are added with new type definitions. The first two fields are of constant length and are at the start of the object, which makes it easy for an implementation to ignore object types that it doesn't recognize.

In general team members have agreed unanimously on the approach to most of the technical issues that arose in the design. Where this has not been the case, the source of the problem lies in the tensions between the Tag Switching and ARIS proposals left unresolved from the architecture deliberations, such as egress versus local control and loop prevention. One such issue that has been resolved is the decision to use TCP as a reliable transport for the protocol instead of building reliability directly into the protocol itself.

The design team's LDP draft has at the time of writing been adopted as a working group document and thus is likely to be the basis of the standard that the WG eventually produces. However, there are plenty of people outside the design team who wish to influence it, and several open issues are yet to be resolved. We discuss these issues in Section 8.5.3.

8.5 **Open Issues**

Although a mass of detail remains to be added before the architecture specification will be finished, it is possible to see that significant progress has been made up to this point. In most cases, "progress" can be loosely defined as the reconciliation of the Tag Switching and the ARIS proposals. A few differences remain to be resolved, however. Unfortunately, these are quite significant differences, or are perceived as being so by the protagonists (who are by no means only Cisco or IBM employees). This section examines each of these major issues. Background on the technical issues behind these debates can be found in Section 7.4.

8.5.1 *Looping*

As pointed out in Section 7.4.1, there are significant differences between the Tag Switching and ARIS approaches with regard to the problem of looping. In response to some of the criticisms leveled at their earlier approach, IBM has proposed a loop prevention scheme that encompasses route pinning with a diffusion computation to ascertain if paths are loop-free. The procedures are in response to routing transients. A description of this mechanism is included in the architecture draft.

One might assume, given that a mechanism for insuring loop freedom is included in the draft, that there should be no issue. Unfortunately the problem is not the mechanism itself. It is not even whether ensuring loop freedom is necessary or not—the authors seem to have agreed that it should be optional. The debate, as near as we can judge, seems to be about exactly what it means for loop prevention to be optional. One interpretation is that all LSRs must implement loop prevention but that it may be turned on or off at the discretion of the network administrator. Another interpretation is that LSRs are not required to implement behavior that is optional. One could claim that an LSR without the ability to perform loop prevention is exactly the same as one that can but has it (optionally) turned off. The architecture claims that both of these schemes can exist interoperably in a network.

It is hard to predict how this issue will be resolved. Perhaps a rough consensus will emerge from the working group, or perhaps intervention from the IETF's area director for routing will be needed to break the deadlock.

It can be argued that the root of this problem is philosophical rather than technical. As discussed in Section 7.4.1, the trade-offs between loop prevention and mitigation are quite complex. While no one thinks loops are a good idea, mitigation is the accepted solution with almost all current network layer routing protocols. Clearly looping cannot be allowed to persist indefinitely or to cause network crashes, but it is not clear that an MPLS network needs to make stronger guarantees of loop freedom than a conventional IP network. However, some participants in the MPLS group argue that the characteristics of MPLS networks are sufficiently different from existing IP networks that loop prevention rather than mitigation is warranted.

8.5.2 *Local Versus Egress Control*

As with the looping issue, the debate over local versus egress control has generated its share of controversy. This debate covers one of the more significant differences between ARIS and Tag Switching, discussed in more detail in Section 7.4.2: the use of ordered or independent binding. Recall that Tag Switching uses the independent (local control) model: an LSR makes a decision to create and advertise a binding without waiting to receive a binding from a neighbor for the same FEC. In ARIS, by contrast, an LSR waits for a binding from its downstream neighbor before allocating a label and advertising it upstream. This is the ordered, or egress controlled, model.

Again, as with looping, the MPLS architecture specifies both mechanisms and explains how they can interwork.

It seems that there are three choices. An LSR could

- Support both egress and local control
- Support egress control only
- Support local control only

The first option is probably the most complex, involving more code, more testing, and more configuration than only supporting one mode. Because there are strong proponents for both egress and local control, however, it seems likely that the support of both egress and local control will remain in the MPLS architecture.

8.5.3 *Label Distribution Issues*

Although we have already looked at LDP, there are other possible techniques for label distribution. There is a debate about whether label distribution should be piggybacked on other protocols when this is possible, done inside LDP in all cases, or done using a combination of the two techniques. In the case of multicast, Cisco has proposed that the Protocol Independent Multicast (PIM) protocol be used to carry labels, as described in Section 5.1.3. A design team, with members from Cisco and IBM, is working on a proposal to carry labels inside RSVP messages to enable labels to be bound to RSVP flows, as described in Section 5.1.5. This will allow one protocol to simultaneously make resource reservations and set up label switched paths for application level flows. This proposal has been adopted as a working draft by the MPLS WG. There is, however, considerable support within the working group for the idea that some "simple" QoS mechanisms are needed in LDP itself, which seems to be a reasonable approach, given that RSVP is not the only method for allocating QoS resources in IP networks. Thus, although RSVP can be used for RSVP flows, other, more coarse-grained QoS capabilities can be supported by LDP. Such support would be more along the lines of "differentiated services," another piece of ongoing IETF work.

On a related note, there is also a proposal to use RSVP as a protocol for setting up explicitly routed label switched paths, rather than using LDP. The reasoning behind this is that, outside of the MPLS group, a proposal has been made to enable an RSVP session to follow an explicitly chosen route. Combining this with the ability to bind labels to RSVP flows would enable explicitly routed label switched paths to be set up with minimal new protocol design. It would also enable resource reservations to be made for the explicitly routed paths.

Various objections have been raised to this approach. These include the fact that it is outside the design goals of RSVP and that it requires an additional protocol. This is also a moderately complex protocol that many vendors have not implemented, and have no desire to implement, and that some network operators seem unwilling to deploy, at least as a general purpose reservation mechanism. To say that there has been lively debate on these matters in the IETF would be something of an understatement.

At the time of writing, there seems little doubt that the LDP will ultimately contain both explicit routing and some mechanism to signal for "non–best effort" service. The challenge will be to provide support for these features without turning it into a "kitchen sink" protocol.

8.6 Summary

Significant progress has been made in defining an architecture for MPLS, although considerably more detail needs to be supplied. Work is underway to define label distribution via LDP and modifications to other protocols. As progress gets made with LDP it will be possible to build the first MPLS LSRs.

There are many details and a smaller number of major issues still unresolved. The necessity for loop prevention and the use of independent or ordered label binding are examples of major issues. Even if these debates are not decisively resolved, MPLS can be made to work, at the cost of some extra complexity in dealing with optional behavior.

We have high hopes that common sense will prevail and that the MPLS working group will converge on a simple, robust, and scalable solution to the problems that we have outlined in this book. We fully expect that solution to help to allow graceful migration of IP networks to supporting new features and levels of service. As to how long it will take to achieve this solution we are uncertain. Looking back at how long it has taken to come this far, it seems safe to assume that the MPLS working group will still be in business in 1999. We do, however, expect to see interoperable MPLS implementations well before then.

Further Reading

The MPLS WG charter can be found on the IETF's home page at

> *www.ietf.org/html.charters/mpls-charter.html*

There is also an MPLS Web page at

> *www.employees.org/~mpls*

Minutes and presentations from the working group meetings can be found via links on this page.

The various working group drafts can also be found on the MPLS page or in the usual Internet drafts directories:

> *ftp://ds.internic.net/internet-drafts*

In contrast to the framework document, the material in the architecture document is, in some cases, presented at a highly detailed level. It rewards careful study, and we recommend it heartily, though it is somewhat hard going and may need to be read several times.

Bibliography

Braden, R., L. Zhang, S. Berson, S. Herzog, and S. Jamin. *Resource ReSerVation Protocol (RSVP): Version 1 Functional Specification.* RFC 2209, September 1997.

Brodnik, A., S. Carlsson, M. Degermark, and S. Pink. "Small Forwarding Tables for Fast Routing Lookups." In Proceedings of ACM SIGCOMM 97, Cannes, France, September 1997.

Chandranmenon, C., and G. Varghese, "Trading Packet Headers for Packet Processing." In Proceedings of ACM SIGCOMM 95, September 1995, 162–173.

Comer, D. E. *Internetworking with TCP/IP. Vol. 1: Principles, Protocols and Architecture.* 3rd ed. Englewood Cliffs, NJ: Prentice-Hall, 1995.

Deering, S., D. Estrin, D. Farinucci, V. Jacobson, C. Gung Liu, and L. Wei. "An Architecture for Wide-area Multicast Routing." In Proceedings of ACM SIGCOMM 94, London, September 1994.

Estrin, D., et al. *Protocol Independent Multicast-Sparse Mode (PIM-SM): Protocol Specification.* RFC 2117, June 1997.

Garcia-Luna-Aceves, J. J. "A Unified Approach to Loop-free Routing Using Distance Vectors or Link States." *Computer Communications Review* 19, no. 4, September 1989.

Halabi, B. *Internet Routing Architectures.* Indianapolis: Cisco Press, 1997.

Heinanen, J. *Multiprotocol Encapsulation over AAL5.* RFC 1483, July 1993.

Huitema, C. *Routing in the Internet.* Englewood Cliffs, NJ: Prentice-Hall, 1995.

Katsube, Y., K. Nagami, and H. Esaki. *Toshiba's Router Architecture Extensions for ATM: Overview.* RFC 2098, April 1997.

Laubach, M. *Classical IP and ARP over ATM.* RFC 1577, January 1994.

Lin, S., and N. McKeown. "A Simulation Study of IP Switching." In Proceedings of ACM SIGCOMM 97, Cannes, France, September 1997.

Moy, J. *OSPF Version 2*. RFC 1583, March 1994.

Nagami, K., et al. *Toshiba's Flow Attribute Notification Protocol (FANP) Specification*. RFC 2129, April 1997.

Newman, P., T. Lyon, and G. Minshall. "Flow Labelled IP: A Connectionless Approach to ATM." In Proceedings of the IEEE Infocom, March 1996.

Newman, P., T. Lyon, and G. Minshall. "IP Switching: ATM Under IP." *IEEE/ACM Transactions on Networking*. Forthcoming.

Newman, P., G. Minshall, T. Lyon, and L. Huston. "IP Switching and Gigabit Routers." *IEEE Communications Magazine* (January 1997).

Paxson, V. "End-to-End Routing Behavior in the Internet." *IEEE/ACM Transactions on Networking* 5 (October 1997): 601–615.

Perlman, R. *Interconnections: Bridges and Routers*. Reading, MA: Addison-Wesley, 1992.

Peterson, L., and B. Davie. *Computer Networks: A Systems Approach*. San Francisco: Morgan Kaufmann, 1996.

Rekhter, Y., B. Davie, D. Katz, E. Rosen, and G. Swallow. *Cisco Systems' Tag Switching Architecture Overview*. RFC 2105, February 1997.

Rekhter, Y., B. Davie, E. Rosen, G. Swallow, D. Farinacci, and D. Katz. "Tag Switching Architecture Overview." In Proceedings of the IEEE 82, no. 12, December 1997, 1973–1983.

Rekhter, Y., and T. Li. *A Border Gateway Protocol 4 (BGP-4)*. RFC 1771, March 1995.

Waldvogel, M., G. Varghese, J. Turner, and B. Plattner. "Scalable High Speed IP Routing Lookups." In Proceedings of ACM SIGCOMM 97, Cannes, France, September 1997.

Glossary

AAL (ATM adaptation layer). A protocol layer that allows higher layer protocols to run over ATM virtual circuits. Of particular relevance is AAL5, which enables segmentation and reassembly of variable-length packets so that they may be sent as streams of cells on an ATM VC.

ARIS (Aggregate Route-based IP Switching). The name given to the label switching scheme invented at IBM, which associates labels with aggregate routes (e.g., address prefixes) in the common case. Also used as the name for the associated label binding distribution protocol.

ATMARP (Asynchronous Transfer Mode Address Resolution Protocol). The server-based protocol that enables IP addresses to be translated into ATM addresses.

BGP (Border Gateway Protocol). The predominant interdomain routing protocol used in IP networks.

BOF (Birds of a Feather). The name for a session at the IETF that is held prior to the formation of a working group to determine whether sufficient interest exists.

BUS (Broadcast and Unknown Server). A server used in emulated LANs to provide broadcast service on a network such as ATM that does not natively support it.

CSR (Cell Switching Router). The name for a device implementing Toshiba's label switching scheme.

Edge LSR. A Label Switching Router (LSR) that first applies a label to a packet.

Egress identifier. A concept used in ARIS, originally referring to the identifier of the last LSR in a label switched path. It has become more of a catchall term for the identifier of an FEC.

FANP (Flow Attribute Notification Protocol). The protocol used by CSRs to notify neighbors that a flow has been selected for switching.

FEC (Forwarding Equivalence Class). A set of packets that can be handled equivalently for the purposes of forwarding and thus is suitable for binding to a single label. The set of packets destined for one address prefix in one example of an FEC. A flow (see below) is another example.

Flow. Generally, a set of packets traveling between a pair of hosts, or a pair of transport protocol ports on a pair of hosts. For example, packets with the same value of <source address, source port, destination address, destination port> might be considered a flow.

Flow identifier. An object used in data-driven approaches (CSR and IP Switching) to define a flow to be label switched.

Forwarding. The process of transferring a packet from an input to an output on either a switch or a router.

GSMP (General Switch Management Protocol). The protocol defined by Ipsilon to allow communication between an IP Switch controller and an ATM switch.

Hard state. State that will remain in place until explicitly deleted, not requiring any periodic refreshing.

In band. Signalling information sent on the same channel (e.g., VC) as data.

IETF (Internet Engineering Task Force). The major standards-setting body for the Internet and the IP suite of protocols.

IFMP (Ipsilon Flow Management Protocol). The label binding protocol for IP Switching, which an IP Switch uses to notify its neighbors that a flow has been selected for label switching.

IP Switch. Defined in this book as a device implementing the Ipsilon approach to label switching. In other settings, may sometimes mean any label switching device that uses IP control protocols or even any device that forwards IP packets (such as an IP router).

IP Switching. Ipsilon's approach to label switching. See IP Switch.

ISR (Integrated Switch Router). The ARIS term for a Label Switching Router.

Label. A short, fixed-length identifier that is used to determine the forwarding of a packet using the exact match algorithm and which is usually rewritten during forwarding.

Label binding. An association between a label and an FEC, which may be advertised to neighbors to establish a label switched path.

Label switching. The generic term used here to describe all approaches to forwarding IP (or other network layer) packets using a label swapping forwarding algorithm under the control of network layer routing algorithms. Label swapping forwarding uses exact match and rewrites the label on forwarding.

LDP (Label Distribution Protocol). The protocol to distribute label bindings being defined by the IETF.

LIS (logical IP subnet). A set of IP nodes connected to an ATM network that share the same subnet address and may thus communicate without the intervention of a router.

LLC/SNAP. A form of encapsulation that enables several higher layer protocols to be multiplexed onto a single datalink, such as an ATM VC.

Longest match. The forwarding algorithm most often used for IP forwarding, in which a (fixed-length) IP address is compared against the (variable-length) entries in a routing table, looking for the entry that matches the most leading bits in the address.

LSR (Label Switching Router). The general term for a device that implements label switching as defined above.

MARS (multicast address resolution server). Device used in ATM networks to enable IP multicast to be mapped onto ATM point-to-multipoint VCs.

MPLS (Multiprotocol Label Switching). The name of the IETF working group that is standardizing label switching.

MTU (maximum transmission unit). The largest packet size that can be transmitted on a datalink without fragmentation.

NHRP (Next Hop Resolution Protocol). Protocol used to enable cut-through paths to be established between logical IP subnets on an ATM network.

OSPF (open shortest path first). Popular link-state routing protocol.

Out of band. Signalling information sent on a channel (e.g., VC) different from that data is sent on.

PIM (Protocol Independent Multicast). Multicast routing protocol being standardized in the IETF.

Port. (1) A physical interface to a switch or router. (2) An identifier used by transport protocols to distinguish application flows between a pair of hosts.

RFC (Request for Comments). A document in a series maintained by the IETF, which includes all Internet protocol standards.

RSVP (Resource Reservation Protocol). Protocol for reserving network resources to provide Quality of Service guarantees to application flows.

Soft state. State that will time out (be deleted) if not periodically refreshed; may be explicitly deleted also, but does not need to be.

Tag. Another name for a label, used in Cisco's Tag Switching.

TCP (Transmission Control Protocol). The widely used reliable byte stream delivery protocol.

TDP (Tag Distribution Protocol). Cisco's label binding distribution protocol.

TFIB (Tag Forwarding Information Base). The data structure used in Tag Switching to hold information about incoming and outgoing tags and the associated FECs.

TSR (Tag Switching Router). The Tag Switching term for an LSR.

VCI (virtual circuit identifier). Field in the ATM header used to identify the virtual circuit to which a cell belongs.

VCID. Identifier used in CSR/FANP to allow two CSRs to refer to a VC using a common value.

VPI (virtual path identifier). Field in the ATM header used to identify the virtual path to which a cell belongs.

Index

About the Authors

Bruce Davie is a technical leader at Cisco Systems, in Chelmsford, Massachusetts, where he manages a group working on the development of Tag Switching, MPLS, and other internetworking technologies. In his previous position as chief scientist at Bell Communications Research, he was responsible for research on gigabit networks, IP version 6, and IP over ATM. The author of *Computer Networks: A Systems Approach* (with Larry Peterson), numerous journal articles, conference papers, and book chapters, Dr. Davie is an active member of both the End-to-End Research Group and the Internet Engineering Task Force (IETF). He is a senior member of the IEEE.

Paul Doolan is chief technology officer with Ennovate Networks in Boxboro, Massachusetts, a start-up company that is embracing MPLS as one of its core technologies. In his previous position at Cisco Systems, Mr. Doolan worked with (among others) Bruce Davie and Yakov Rekhter on the Tag Switching proposals. An active member of the MPLS working group, he is co-author of the MPLS Framework and Label Distribution Protocol documents. This is his first book.

Yakov Rekhter works at Cisco Systems, where he is a Cisco Fellow. He was one of the principal architects of the Tag Switching proposal and is an active participant in the MPLS working group. Prior to coming to Cisco he spent over 10 years with IBM at the T. J. Watson Research Center.

Yakov was one of the leading architects, as well as a major software developer, of the NSFNET Backbone Phase II. He is one of the leading designers of the Border Gateway Protocol (BGP). In addition to MPLS he actively participates in many activities of the Internet Engineering Task Force (IETF). From 1993 until 1997 he was a member of the Internet Architecture Board (IAB). Currently he is a chairman of the Inter-Domain Routing (IDR) Working Group of the IETF. He is the author or co-author of 37 RFCs, as well as numerous presentations, papers, and articles on TCP/IP and the Internet.